# *Study and Revise*
# GCSE
# Spanish

## Ana Kolkowska

## Acknowledgements

The author and publishers would like to thank the following examination boards for permission to reproduce the following specimen exam material.

Northern Examinations and Assessment Board GCSE Spanish Specimen Material 1998 Examination: Listening Foundation Section A Questions 1–3, 5, 7–15 in Chapter 12 **pp. 126–7** Listening exercises 1–13, Question 6 in Chapter 5 **p. 40** Foundation Task 1, Higher Questions 4–14 in Chapter 12 **pp. 128–9** Listening exercises 14–24; Speaking Foundation and Higher Role Play 2 in Chapter 8 **p. 65** Higher Task 2; Reading Foundation Questions 1–5 in Chapter 12 **pp. 131–3** Reading exercises 1–5, Question 6 in Chapter 10 **p. 77** Foundation Task 3, Question 9 in Chapter 12 **p. 133** Reading exercise 6, Higher Question 1 in Chapter 7 **p. 59** Higher Task 3, Questions 2, 4, 5, 8, and 10 in Chapter 12 **pp. 133–5** Reading exercises 8–12; Writing Higher Question 2 in Chapter 12 **p. 136** Writing exercise 4.

EDEXCEL London Examinations – Modern Foreign Languages Spanish Specimen Papers & Mark Schemes G7/6: Paper 1F Listening and Responding Questions 12–16 in Chapter 1 **p. 10** Foundation Task 2 and Questions 30–34 in Chapter 10 **p. 76** Foundation Task 1, Paper 1H Listening and Responding Questions 26–31 in Chapter 10 **p. 80** Higher Task 1; Paper 2F and 2H Speaking Role Play A (1) in Chapter 12 **p. 130** Speaking exercise 1, Role Play C3 in Chapter 12 **p. 130** Speaking exercise 4; Paper 3F Reading and Responding Question 6 in Chapter 10 **p. 77** Foundation Task 3; Paper 4H Writing Question 2 in Chapter 9 **p. 73** Higher Task 3. Edexcel Foundation, London Examinations accepts no responsibility whatsoever for the accuracy or method of working in the answers given.

Reproduced by kind permission of the Midland Examining Group Specimen Question Papers and Mark Schemes (June 1998 onwards) printed June 1995 © MEG (not including third party copyright material): Listening Section 1 Exercise 3 Questions 7–11 in Chapter 8 **p. 63** Foundation Task 1, Section 2 Exercise 1 Questions 1–5 in Chapter 9 **p. 73** Higher Task 1, Exercise 2 Question 6 in Chapter 3 **p. 24** Foundation Task 1, Exercise 3 Question 11 in Chapter 7 **p. 55** Foundation Task 1. Speaking Role Play 1, Card 1 in Chapter 7 **p. 55** Foundation Task 2, Card 2 in Chapter 8 **p. 63** Foundation Task 2, Card 3 in Chapter 12 **p. 130** Speaking exercise 2, Card 4 in Chapter 6 **p. 48** Foundation Task 2, Role Play 2, Card 1 in Chapter 12 **p. 130** Speaking exercise 3, Card 4 in Chapter 7 **p. 58** Higher Task 2. Reading Section 1, Exercise 1, Questions 3–4 in Chapter 7 **p. 55** Foundation Task 3, Section 2, Exercise 1, Questions 1–8 in Chapter 4 **p. 36** Higher Task 2. Writing Foundation Section 1 Questions 1–2 in Chapter 12 **p. 136** Writing exercises 1–2, Section 2 Question 1 in Chapter 9 **p. 70** Foundation Task 2, Higher Section 2 Question 2 in Chapter 10 **p. 81** Higher Task 4. The Midland Examining Group bears no responsibility for the example answers to questions taken from its past and specimen question papers which are contained in this publication.

Southern Examining Group 1998 Examinations Spanish Modular Specimen Papers and Marking Schemes (issued January 1996): Module 1 Reading Task 5 in Chapter 9 **p. 73** Higher Task 2, Listening Task 5 in Chapter 9 **p. 69** Foundation Task 1; Module 2 Listening Higher Question 2 in Chapter 8 **p. 65** Higher Task 1; Module 3 Writing Higher Task 3 in Chapter 7 **p. 59** Higher Task 4; Module 4 Listening Higher Question 1 in Chapter 2 **p. 20** Higher Task 2, Higher Question 3 in Chapter 3 **p. 27** Higher Task 1, Speaking Higher Tier only (page 142) in Chapter 10 **p. 80** Higher Task 2.

Text © Ana Maria Kolkowska 2004

First published in this edition 2004
exclusively for WHSmith by
Hodder & Stoughton Educational
338 Euston Road
London NW1 3BH

Impression number    10 9 8 7 6 5 4 3 2 1
Year        2010 2009 2008 2007 2006 2005 2004

Prepared by *specialist* publishing services, Milton Keynes

Printed and bound in the UK by Scotprint

A CIP record for this book is available from the British Library

ISBN 0 340 85869 9

# Contents

# Contents

## How will this book help me?

This *Study and Revise GCSE Spanish* book covers ten topics, and includes vocabulary and structures that you need to achieve good grades at GCSE for any of the exam boards. It presents the language in a way that is easy to grasp and to remember.

Find out from the start which tiers you have been entered for so that you can see which sections of the revision guide will be most useful to you. For example, you might be entered for Higher Listening, Speaking and Reading and Foundation Writing.

## Use the Checklist and Notes/Options

Work through each chapter: shade in or tick the Checklist (Fine or Help!). Then read through the Notes/Options paying particular attention to the items where you have shaded or ticked Help! and where you need to build your confidence. Once you have worked through the Notes/Options, have a go at the Test yourself exercises at the end of each chapter tier. There are exercises within all four skills areas: Listening, Speaking, Reading, Writing.

Mark your answers using the key in the shaded boxes. If you haven't got a very good mark, check back to the chapter again.

## A practice mock exam

Finally there is a mock exam in Chapter 12 that is a compilation of specimen exam questions taken from various exam boards. Follow the instructions given at the beginning of each section of the mock exam and try to complete the chapter in conditions as near as possible to a real exam. It is not a good idea, however, to do the whole mock exam in one sitting. Make sure you have breaks after each section.

When you have finished the Listening, Reading, Speaking and Writing sections mark your answers. Take special care over the Writing and Speaking mark schemes. They are complicated but knowing the standards demanded by the exam boards will help you achieve the grade you want.

## A grammar reference

You will find the grammar explanations in Chapter 13 very useful as your revision progresses.

## Train your memory

Plan out the time before your exam so that you revise a little every day, allowing your mind to absorb the information. Give more time to the topics that you find most difficult. Bear in mind the other subjects you are taking; juggle your revision time carefully.

Some people find that they are most receptive to learning and memorising in the mornings, but only you can decide what works best for you. Be aware of what are the hardest topics and structures for you, and don't leave them to the last minute!

### TOP TEN TIPS for learning vocabulary

1   Use different coloured pens to highlight masculine and feminine words.

2   Draw an item or symbol for key vocabulary.

3   Don't try to learn more than ten words at a time.

4   Take ten minutes to draw a spider diagram. Then, after a break, take another ten minutes to write out the vocabulary as a list.

5   Use a list of ten words, start at the bottom and work upwards, as well as downwards.

6   Visualise each item of vocabulary as you say the word in Spanish.

7   Record yourself – play it back and imagine the item again.

8   Ask friends and family to test you on vocabulary.

9   Remember that with regular effort you can build a bigger vocabulary and recall it.

10  Think positive. Vocabulary is the key and the more often you learn small chunks, the easier it gets.

## Are you sitting comfortably?

You need to be at ease when you are revising. Here are some tips to help you choose an ideal working environment.

**LOCATION**  Never revise in the kitchen or the living room with the TV on or with brothers or sisters around. Find a place that is quiet and where there are no distractions. If you find it hard to revise at home, you could go to your library.

**LIGHTING**  Natural light is best. If you can, sit by a window, If you have to work in artificial light, try to use a lamp rather than fluorescent lighting as this can give you eye strain. Avoid shadows; make sure that the light comes from your left if you are right-handed, and from your right if you are left-handed.

**HEATING**  If you are too warm while you are revising, you might find that you start falling asleep – not ideal for training your memory! Fresh air helps concentration so open the windows while you are working, or at least during your short breaks.

**SPACE**  Organise your desk or table so that your books, notes, dictionaries, pens and paper are within easy reach. If you have to keep getting up to look for things you will be easily distracted.

**POSITION** Make sure your chair is at the right height and that it is keeping your back straight while you are revising. You might get back-ache if you sit awkwardly. Never work in an armchair or lying on your bed: you will be too relaxed to take much in!

**FUEL** Meals are very important. Pay as much attention to your food intake as does an athlete training for a competition! Limit the amount of sugary and fatty things you eat as these increase irritability and can disrupt concentration. Likewise, stimulating drinks (such as coffee and tea) can revive you in the short term, but they might also disturb your sleep pattern and affect your memory if you're tired.

## During the exam

- Structure your time so that you have enough time to answer all of the questions. Don't spend too long on one question. First answer the questions you can do easily and then go back to the more difficult ones.

- Answer all the questions.

- Look carefully at the number of marks you can get for each question. For example three marks means you must give three items of information in your answer.

- Stick to the point. Give opinions and reasons wherever you can and use the different tenses where appropriate. Don't pad out your answer with irrelevant material, it will be obvious that you can't answer the question.

- Plan your answers, especially for the Writing paper. Draw a quick spider diagram.

- Write clearly. Ask for some blank sheets if you want to write out notes or plan using a spider diagram. Remember to cross out neatly any work you don't want the examiner to mark.

- Leave some time at the end to look over your answers and for a final dictionary check.

- Remember to answer in the correct language!

**For your own notes**

........................................................     ........................................................

........................................................     ........................................................

........................................................     ........................................................

........................................................     ........................................................

........................................................     ........................................................

........................................................     ........................................................

........................................................     ........................................................

## Rubrics and instructions

Here is a list of the types of rubrics and instructions you might come across in the exam papers. Familiarise yourself with them as failing to understand instructions might mean lost marks.

### All papers

|  |  |
|---|---|
| Primero ... | = First ... |
| Ahora ... | = Now ... |
| En español | = In Spanish |
| En inglés | = In English |
| En cifras | = In numbers |
| Verdadero/Cierto | = True |
| Falso | = False |
| Ejemplo | = Example |
| Las respuestas siguientes | = The following answers, etc. |
| Algunas preguntas/frases | = Some questions/sentences etc. |
| Para cada pregunta/persona/cliente, etc. | = For each question/person/customer, etc. |
| Habla/escribe sobre/de ... | = Talk/Write about ... |
| *Question words such as:* | |
| ¿Qué? | = What? |
| ¿Dónde? | = Where? |
| ¿Quién? | = Who? |
| ¿Cuánto? | = How much? |
| ¿Cuándo? | = When? |
| ¿Cómo? | = How/What? |
| Busca las palabras/frases/los errores, etc. | = Find the words/sentences/mistakes, etc. |
| Cada una de estas frases contiene un error. | = Each of these phrases contains a mistake. |
| Contesta en español o pon una señal (√) en las casillas. | = Answer in Spanish or tick the boxes. |
| Contesta (a) las preguntas. | = Answer the questions. |
| Completa el cuadro/las frases/la lista/la descripción/el formulario. | = Complete the box/phrases/list/description/form. |
| Copia ... | = Copy ... |

|  |  |
|---|---|
| Corrige los errores/las palabras subrayadas. | = Correct the mistakes/underlined words. |
| Cuenta ... | = Tell ... |
| Da la vuelta. | = Turn over. |
| Ejemplo | = Example |
| Empareja ... | = Match up ... |
| En cada casilla pon el número del párrafo/de la frase/de la pregunta/de la palabra que corresponde a ... | = In each box put the number of the paragraph/phrase/question/word which corresponds to ... |
| Escoge la descripción que corresponde mejor ... | = Choose the description that best fits ... |
| Escribe la letra/el número ... | = Write the letter/number ... |
| Escribe las respuestas ... | = Write the answers ... |
| Escribe la letra que corresponde. | = Write the letter which matches. |
| Haz unos apuntes/una lista. | = Make notes/a list. |
| Identifica | = Identify |
| Indica sí o no. | = Indicate yes or no. |
| La palabra subrayada no es correcta. Escribe la palabra correcta. | = The underlined word is not correct. Write the correct word. |
| Lee las preguntas/la lista, etc. | = Read the questions/the list, etc. |
| Llena las casillas/los huecos. | = Fill the boxes/gaps. |
| Mira los apuntes/los dibujos, etc. | = Look at the notes/pictures, etc. |
| No necesitarás todas las letras. | = You will not need all the letters. |
| Ordena para indicar ... | = Put in the correct order to show ... |
| Pon una señal (√) en la casilla correcta/más adecuada. | = Tick the correct/appropriate box. |
| Pon una señal (√) al lado de sólo 5 letras/casillas. | = Tick only 5 letters/boxes. |
| Rellena los blancos/espacios. | = Fill in the blanks. |
| Si la frase/afirmación es verdad(era), pon una señal (√) en la casilla Verdadero. | = If the statement is correct, tick the True box. |
| Sólo una de estas frases es correcta. | = Only one of these phrases is correct. |
| Subraya ... | = Underline ... |
| Tienes que ... | = You have to ... |

# Tricks of the trade to make the grade!

## Listening

¿Dónde se pueden oír estas frases?

| | |
|---|---|
| Entre dos personas | = Between two people |
| Escucha (atentamente) ... | = Listen (carefully) ... |
| Está hablando con ... | = He/She is talking to ... |
| Estás oyendo ... | = You are listening to ... |
| Habrá dos pausas durante el anuncio/extracto. | = There will be two pauses during the advert/extract. |
| ¿Quién habla? | = Who is speaking? |
| Vas a oír ... | = You are going to hear ... |
| ... un mensaje/una conversación/ un diálogo/un programa/un reportaje/una entrevista/ un interviú | = ... a message/ conversation/ dialogue/programme/ report/account/ interview |
| ... en la radio/televisión, etc. | = on the radio/television, etc. |
| Vas a oír la conversación dos veces. | = You are going to hear the conversation twice. |

## Reading

¿Dónde se pueden leer estas frases?

| | |
|---|---|
| Lee (atentamente) ... | = Read (carefully) ... |
| He aquí ... | = Here is ... |
| ... una lista/alguna información/ una postal/una carta/ unos anuncios/un texto/ un extracto | = ... a list/some information/a postcard/a letter/ some adverts/a text/an extract |
| ... de un periódico/una revista, etc. | = ... from a news-paper/magazine, etc. |

## Speaking

| | |
|---|---|
| Contesta (a) la pregunta de ... | = Answer ...'s question |
| Da las gracias ... | = Thank ... |
| Decide cómo | = Decide how |
| Di ... | = Say ... |
| Explica ... | = Explain ... |
| He aquí lo que tienes que pedir o decir (*) y lo que tienes que preguntar (?). | = This is what you must ask for or say (*) and what you must ask (?). |
| Preséntate | = Introduce yourself |
| Saluda ... | = Greet ... |

## Writing

| | |
|---|---|
| Contesta (a) todas las preguntas. | = Answer all the questions. |
| Escribe ... | = Write ... |
| ... una lista/una postal/una carta/ un artículo/un reportaje/ las cosas etc. | = ... a list/postcard/ letter/article/report/ the things etc. |
| Escribe unas ... palabras. | = Write about ... words. |
| Estás enviando ... | = You are sending ... |
| Describe ... | = Describe ... |
| Dile lo que has ... | = Tell him/her what you have ... |
| Incluye la siguiente información. | = Include the following information. |
| Quieres escribir a ... | = You want to write to ... |
| Rellena el formulario. | = Fill in the form. |

**CONTEXT** Make sure you understand the question; it might ask you for details or for a general impression. When you are reading or listening to a section keep an eye or an ear out for the words which will actually answer the question – you can almost ignore the rest. If you don't understand a word, try to work out what it means from its context. The rest of the words in the sentence will give you clues.

**STRUCTURE** Use your knowledge of grammar structure; look for tenses, plurals and adjectives to help you work out what a sentence is about.

**SPANISH LIFESTYLE** Use your knowledge of Spanish life and customs. For example, you may know that the Spanish have dinner late in the evening. For a question asking you what time a Spaniard has dinner, knowing that the answer will most likely be a later time than is usual in Britain will help you listen out for an appropriate time.

**TRAPS** Look out for words which are similar in English and Spanish such as *la policía* (police) and *el tráfico* (traffic). Look out also for differences in Spanish and English spellings as in the following examples: *foto* (photo), *estudiar* (to study), *teatro* (theatre), *catedral* (cathedral). But beware of words that are similar in both languages but have different meanings, as with, for example, *simpático* which means friendly in Spanish.

**BRIDGES** If you don't understand a word, look at its construction; what is at the beginning and at the end of the word? For example, you may not know the word *carnicería*, but if you recognise that *carne* means meat and that *-ería* on the end of a word indicates the shop where the item is sold, you can work out that *carnicería* means butcher's.

**INITIATIVE** If you can't remember a word, especially in the Writing and Speaking papers, don't invent one or use an English word. Try to get round it by using other Spanish words and phrases, for example, *tienda grande* instead of *grandes almacenes* and *necesito folletos* rather than *le ruego me mande folletos*.

## The mock exam

### Before you start

1   Can you understand the Spanish instructions? If not, look at the Rubrics and instructions on page 3 of this section.

2   Have you got ready the following items: clock, at least two good pens and plenty of paper for notes and ideas?

3   Listening Paper: have you got the CD in the machine and can you find the right track?

4   Speaking Test: have you got a blank cassette in another machine to enable you to record your answers and mark yourself? If this is not possible, ask a friend to mark you, or mark yourself after each question so that you don't forget what you have said.

### During the mock exam

**INSTRUCTIONS** Follow the instructions at the beginning of each section carefully.

**TIME** Give yourself the stated time allotted for using the dictionary as instructed.

**SHOW OFF** Make sure you show you can use past and future tenses as well as present tenses.

**TAKE A BREAK** Give yourself a break after each paper!

## What's my grade?

If you want to know what grade you have achieved in the mock exam, follow this scheme.

How do I add up my totals? Each paper is worth 25% of the total score. Use a calculator to help you work out your scores for each paper. You must add up the marks for the questions you were required to do and turn the total into a percentage.

For the Speaking Test add together your totals for the role plays and then turn the total into a percentage.

Add up the total for each of the four papers (Listening, Speaking, Reading, Writing) and divide the result by 4 to get your final percentage.

How do I turn the totals into a percentage? If you have a pocket calculator enter your total marks for the section, divide by the maximum marks for the section and multiply by 100. The answer is your percentage for that test. For example: $18 \div 25 \times 100 = 72\%$. The percentages are then converted to a final grade.

| Foundation | | Higher | |
|---|---|---|---|
| Grade | % | Grade | % |
| G | 1–20 | D | 1–25 |
| F | 21–40 | C | 26–50 |
| E | 41–60 | B | 51–75 |
| D | 61–80 | A | 76–100 |
| C | 81–100 | | |

## Are you happy with your result?

**¡Enhorabuena!** If you have achieved a result of more than 75% of the total score (Foundation or Higher) and you are happy with your result, you can relax. Just spend half an hour a day doing general reading in Spanish, until a day or two before your exam.

For final revision: look at the Notes/Options for each chapter. Look through the lists and diagrams you have made and the word lists on pages 82–116. Have a final quick read through Chapter 12.

## Are you unhappy with your result?

**Don't despair, follow these guidelines and you will improve your results.**

If you feel that a certain skill has let you down (Listening, Speaking, Reading or Writing), concentrate your revision on improving that skill. If you feel that you have not shown sufficient knowledge of a particular topic, concentrate your revision on that topic. Use the word lists and grammar on pages 82–125 to help you revise. If a poor understanding and use of tenses has let you down, check Chapter 13 (Grammar) and learn the tenses.

If you think you could have got a better grade if you had been able to express opinions and expand on basic points, go back to the Checklists and concentrate your efforts on the Notes/Options that deal with opinions and developing discussion.

## Last minute tips!

### Listening

- Remember that you don't need to write in full sentences.

- Look carefully at the pictures in the questions.

- If you miss a question, don't panic, keep listening, you can have another go in the second listen through.

- Write in the correct language.

- Don't worry too much about spelling as long as your answer is clear.

- If you are required to answer questions in Spanish, you will not be marked for the accuracy of the language.

### Speaking

- Practise your presentation and topics using a cassette recorder and with friends until you can speak confidently and without hesitation.

- Remember that in the exam, once you have spoken, there is not much opportunity to go back and correct what you have said. Nor is it possible to leave a difficult question that you might get till last. It is better to have clear in your mind what you are going to say. Pause for a few moments before you speak and order what you are going to say. Perhaps try to recall a diagram you have made.

- Once you start to speak, do so confidently.

- If you don't understand a question or want something repeated, say so: *No comprendo*, or *Puede repetir, por favor*.

- Try to spot the unexpected in the role plays.

- Remember to give opinions and reasons at every opportunity.

- Try to sound as spontaneous as possible and keep talking. If you rely on the examiner to prompt you with questions you might get asked a question you don't understand!

- Let the conversation flow, don't just answer questions, **ask** questions as well!

### Reading

- Answer in the correct language!

- Marks will not be taken off for incorrect spellings as long as your answer is clear.

- Don't miss out questions. You are more likely to get a mark if you make an intelligent guess rather than leave a gap.

- If you are required to answer questions in Spanish, you will not be marked for the accuracy of the language.

- Don't spend too much time on each question as you might run out of time for other questions. You can always go back to a question when you've gone through the rest of the paper.

### Writing

- Read the questions at least twice before you begin.

- Plan your answer using a flow chart or spider diagram so that you cover all the points required by the question.

- Don't spend too much time on each question as you might run out of time for other questions. You can always go back to a question when you've gone through the rest of the paper.

- Remember to give opinions and reasons at every opportunity.

**Are you ready? ¡Buena suerte!**

*Ana Kolkowska*

## Checklist

**How confident do you feel about these?
Can you:**

| | Fine | Help! |
|---|---|---|
| 1 say and spell your name? | ☐ | ☐ |
| 2 give your nationality? | ☐ | ☐ |
| 3 give your age and birthday? | ☐ | ☐ |
| 4 describe yourself (physical appearance and character)? | ☐ | ☐ |
| 5 give the same details about your family? | ☐ | ☐ |
| 6 talk about your pets (size, number and colour)? | ☐ | ☐ |
| 7 say where you live and spell it out? | ☐ | ☐ |
| 8 say how you feel (ill, well, tired, hungry, thirsty, cold, hot, better)? | ☐ | ☐ |
| 9 say where you have a pain? | ☐ | ☐ |
| 10 ask for items at a chemist's? | ☐ | ☐ |
| 11 call for help? | ☐ | ☐ |

## All about me!

Wherever you have selected Help! in the checklist, make the most of the Notes/Options and the word lists to build your confidence.

*Sábado →*
*← El viaje*
*↑ El instituto*
*Foundation ↘*
*Tiempo libre*
*Higher ↗*

## HELP IS AT HAND!

**Notes/Options**

1 ¿Cómo te llamas?
Me llamo …

¿Cómo se llama usted? = What's your name?(usted)

¿Cómo se escribe tu nombre?
Se escribe - M - I - G - U - E - L. *Make sure you know how to pronounce the alphabet.*

nombre = name
apellido = surname

2 ¿Cuál es tu nacionalidad?
¿Cuál es su nacionalidad? (usted)
Soy inglés/inglesa. escocés/escocesa
irlandés/irlandesa
galés/galesa
*Girls add an 'a' and lose the accent!*

3 ¿Cuántos años tienes?
Tengo 16 años. 16 = dieciséis, not sesenta (60)

edad = age
¿Cuándo es tu cumpleaños? = When is your birthday?

Es el quince de noviembre.

Do you remember all of these months?

| enero | mayo | septiembre |
|---|---|---|
| febrero | junio | octubre |
| marzo | julio | noviembre |
| abril | agosto | diciembre |

fecha de nacimiento = date of birth
4 ¿Cómo eres? = What are you like?
bastante = quite
ni … ni … = neither … nor …
Soy alto/a. alto/a = tall
bajo/a = short
Soy delgado/a. delgado/a = slim
gordo/a = fat
fuerte = strong build
Soy moreno/a. moreno/a = dark (hair and skin)
rubio/a = fair (hair and skin)
negro/a = black
blanco/a = white
mestizo/a = mixed race
pelirrojo/a = redhead

Tengo los ojos castaños/marrones. = I have brown eyes.
azules = blue
verdes = green
negros = dark brown

*When describing your eyes you add an 's' at the end of the colour.*

Tengo el pelo castaño/marrón. = I have brown hair.
rubio = blond
negro = black

Tengo el pelo largo.
largo= long
corto = short
liso = straight
rizado = curly
ondulado = wavy
rapado = shaved

*When describing your hair you add an 'o' at the end of the colour or describing word.*

Soy simpático/a.
simpático/a = friendly
tímido/a = shy
gracioso/a = funny

Tengo buen sentido del humor.
el sentido del humor = sense of humour

5 ¿Tienes hermanos? = Do you have brothers or sisters?

Tengo un hermano mayor y dos hermanas menores.
mayor(es) = older
menor(es) = younger

Soy hijo/a único/a. = I'm an only child.
hermanastro(s) = stepbrother(s)
hermanastra(s) = stepsister(s)

Mi hermano se llama Felipe. Es simpático e inteligente.
*'y' becomes 'e' in front of a word beginning with 'i'.*

Mis hermanas se llaman Elena y María.
se llaman = they are called

Son guapas y artísticas.
guapo/a(s)
= They are attractive and artistic.

Felipe tiene 18 años.
*Not 'Felipe es 18 años'.*

Cristina y María tienen 10 y 12 años.
= Cristina and María are 10 and 12 years old.

*'N' on the end of a verb describes more than one person, i.e. tiene = he/she has, tienen = they have.*

¿Cómo es tu madre/padre?
padre = father
madre = mother
padres = parents

Mi madre se llama Teresa. Es muy trabajadora y cariñosa.
trabajador(a) (es/as) = hard working
cariñoso/a(s) = affectionate

Mi padre se llama Tomás. Es muy tranquilo.
tranquilo/a(s) = calm, easy going

Revise numbers 1–100, make sure you know all the ages of your family!

| | | |
|---|---|---|
| 1 un/uno/una | 11 once | 21 veintiuno |
| 2 dos | 12 doce | 22 veintidós |
| 3 tres | 13 trece | 30 treinta |
| 4 cuatro | 14 catorce | 31 treinta y uno |
| 5 cinco | 15 quince | 40 cuarenta |
| 6 seis | 16 dieciséis | 41 cuarenta y uno |
| 7 siete | 17 diecisiete | 50 cincuenta |
| 8 ocho | 18 dieciocho | 60 sesenta |
| 9 nueve | 19 diecinueve | 70 setenta |
| 10 diez | 20 veinte | 80 ochenta |
| | | 90 noventa |
| | | 100 cien |

*Uno/a becomes un when it is used in front of a masculine singular noun, e.g. Tiene un año.*

6 ¿Tienes un animal en casa? = Do you have a pet?

No, no tengo animales en casa. No tengo mascotas.

Sí, tengo un perro.
un perro = dog
un gato = cat

Se llama Toto. Es blanco y negro. Tiene dos años.

Look at the word list on page 85 to revise animals.

7 ¿Dónde vives?
¿Dónde vive?
= Where do you live? (usted)

Vivo en 49 Park Road.

¿Cómo se escribe? = How do you spell it?

Se escribe P-A-R-K R-O-A-D.
domicilio = address

Listen to the Alphabet on the CD (Chapter 1). Check that you can spell out your name and address. Practise spelling the names of people in your family.

8 ¿Qué tal?/¿Cómo estás?
¿Cómo está?
= How are you? (usted)

¿Cómo te sientes?
¿Cómo se siente?
= How do you feel? (usted)

Estoy bien.

Estoy estupendamente, muy bien, bien, regular, mal, muy mal, fatal.

| | |
|---|---|
| Me siento mal/bien. | = I don't feel well./ I feel well. |
| Estoy enfermo/a. | = I'm ill. |
| Estoy cansado/a. | = I'm tired. |
| Tengo hambre. | = I'm hungry. |
| Tengo sed. | = I'm thirsty. |
| Tengo calor. | = I'm hot. |
| Me siento mejor/peor. | = I feel better/worse. |

Have a look at the word list on page 86 to revise how you feel in more depth!

## HOW'S YOUR MEMORY?

**Talking about age, eyes and hair**

| | |
|---|---|
| Tengo | 16 años |
| Tiene | los ojos castaños |
| Tienen | el pelo corto y liso |

**Describing size and character**

| | |
|---|---|
| Soy | alto/a, bajo/a, delgado/a, fuerte |
| Es | simpático/a |
| Son | inteligentes |

*For girls replace 'o' with 'a' as an ending.*

### Going for a C?

Add simple opinions to your descriptions and give a simple reason why. Use:

odio
no me gusta nada
no me gusta
me gusta
me gusta mucho
me encanta

Learn describing words such as **simpático** and **egoísta** so that you can say why you like or dislike something/somebody.

Revise the parts of the body. Look at the word list on page 87 to help you.

| | |
|---|---|
| **9** ¿Dónde te duele?/¿Dónde le duele? | = Where do you (tú)/ (usted) have a pain? |

*Remember that the tú form is used for talking to family and people your own age and that the usted form is used for talking to older people whom you don't know.*

| | |
|---|---|
| ¿Qué te duele?/¿Qué le duele? | = What hurts? |
| Me duele la cabeza./ Tengo dolor de cabeza. | = I have got a headache. |
| Me duelen las muelas. | *Add an 'n' ending to the verb, because in Spanish you refer to teeth (more than one).* |
| **10** ¿Qué desea?/¿En qué puedo ayudarle? | = How can I help you? |
| ¿Tiene tiritas? | = Do you have any plasters? |
| aspirinas | = aspirins |
| jarabe para la tos | = cough syrup |
| pastillas | = tablets |
| ¿Quiere un paquete/ una caja/una botella grande? | = Do you want a big packet/box/bottle? |
| No, un paquete pequeño. | |
| **11** ¿Necesita ayuda? | = Do you need help? |
| ¡Socorro! | = Help! |

### Test yourself

**Task 1**          Reading

Rellena la ficha con tus datos personales.
(Fill in this form with your personal details.)

NOMBRE: *luisa*

APELLIDO: *manzi*

EDAD: *16 años*

FECHA DE NACIMIENTO: *12 / 12 / 9 0*

DOMICILIO: ..............................

Nº DE TELÉFONO: *020773125199*

### Task 2 — Listening

**LA FAMILIA**

Try this listening question (Chapter 1 Foundation).

In the pauses on the recording, fill in the blanks in your book with the names of people you hear.

Ejemplo: Ana

1 *Montse* ✓
2 *Carlos* ✓
3 *Jorge* ✓
4 *Magdalena* ✓
5 *Luis* ✓

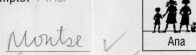

Ana

Jorge | Magdalena

Carlos | Luis | Montse

### Task 3 — Writing

Escribe una carta a tu amigo/a español(a) describiéndote a ti y a tu familia. (Write a short letter to a Spanish friend about you and your family, using 60–80 words.)

Look back at the Checklist.

When you have finished, ask a friend who is also learning Spanish to read it. Can they understand it? Give yourself a point for every detail they understand (e.g. Tengo un hermano. = 1 point).

#### DO YOU REMEMBER THESE?

Letter-writing to a friend:

Start off:     Querido + boy's name
              Querida + girl's name

Finish off:   Un saludo/Abrazos

## Answers

## For your own notes

..................................................................
..................................................................
..................................................................
..................................................................
..................................................................
..................................................................
..................................................................
..................................................................
..................................................................
..................................................................
..................................................................
..................................................................

**11** ¿Te dan dinero tus padres?

= Do you get pocket money?

Me dan 5 libras a la semana.

a la semana = a week

¿En qué te lo gastas?

= What do you spend it on?

¿En qué te gastas el dinero/ la paga?

la paga = pocket money

Me lo gasto en ropa y cosméticos.

= I spend it on clothes and make-up.

Compro videojuegos y CDs.

= I buy video games and CDs.

salir con los amigos

= to go out with friends

Estoy ahorrando para comprar una bici de montaña.

= I'm saving up to buy a mountain bike.

**12** ¿Qué hay para jóvenes en tu barrio?

= What is there to do for young people in your area?

¿Qué hay de interés en tu pueblo?

= What's of interest in your town?

Hay un estadio, campos de tenis y un centro comercial.

= There is a stadium, tennis courts and a shopping centre.

## HOW IS YOUR MEMORY?

| Se puede + infinitive = you can/one can + activity |
|---|
| Se puede + ir de paseo<br>        bailar<br>        ver un partido<br>        jugar al baloncesto |

**13** ¿Qué hiciste el fin de semana pasado?

= What did you do last weekend?

Revise the preterite tense so that you can talk about what you did. See page 141.

| Time Markers | |
|---|---|
| el sábado pasado | = last Saturday |
| anoche | = last night |
| ayer por la tarde | = yesterday afternoon |
| la semana pasada | = last week |

Here are some useful phrases about activities in the preterite tense.

| | |
|---|---|
| fui de compras | = I went shopping |
| jugué al baloncesto | = I played basketball |
| salí con mis amigos | = I went out with my friends |
| vi una película | = I watched a film |
| toqué el saxofón | = I played the saxophone |
| escuché música | = I listened to music |
| monté en bicicleta | = I rode my bike |
| lo pasé bien | = I had a good time |
| me divertí | = I enjoyed myself |

Look at the word lists on pages 91, 93 and 96 for more phrases.

**14** ¿Qué vas a hacer este fin de semana?

= What are you going to do this weekend?

There are two ways to talk about your future plans. You can use voy a + infinitive or the full future tense.

| Voy a + infinitive | |
|---|---|
| voy a visitar a mis abuelos | = I'm going to visit my grandparents |
| voy a estudiar | = I'm going to study |
| voy a ir a la piscina | = I'm going to the swimming-pool |
| lo voy a pasar bien | = I'm going to have a good time |
| me voy a divertir | = I'm going to enjoy myself |

To revise the future tense see page 143.

| | |
|---|---|
| iré | = I will go |
| jugaré | = I will play (game/sport) |
| saldré | = I will go out |
| veré | = I will watch |
| tocaré | = I will play (music/instrument) |
| escucharé | = I will listen |
| montaré | = I will ride |
| lo pasaré bien | = I will have a good time |
| me divertiré | = I will enjoy myself |

| Time Markers | |
|---|---|
| esta tarde | = this afternoon |
| mañana | = tomorrow |
| mañana por la tarde | = tomorrow afternoon |
| este fin de semana | = this weekend |
| el fin de semana próximo | = next weekend |
| la semana que viene | = next week |

## Test yourself

### Task 1 — Listening

Listen to the CD (Chapter 3, Foundation). Play the exercise twice.

Teresa te ha mandado un cassette en el que menciona cinco (5) de sus hobbys. ¿Cuáles son?

Pon una señal ✔ al lado de los cinco (5) hobbys.

Ejemplo

Ahora mira los dibujos.

Ahora escucha a Teresa.

 1    6

 2    7

 3    8

 4    9

 5    10

### Task 2 — Speaking

Time yourself and talk for at least 15 seconds on each of the following topics:

el deporte          la música
la televisión       esta tarde
el cine
el fin de semana pasado
el fin de semana que viene

Use written cheats to help you until you feel that you can talk without hesitating. Can you manage 30 seconds on any of them? ¡Enhorabuena!

### Task 3 — Reading

Read the following letter from a Spanish pen-pal and mark whether the following statements are true or false.

¡Hola!

Me llamo Gabriel. Tengo 15 años y vivo en Vitoria. Me gustan mucho los deportes. Juego al tenis dos veces a la semana y practico el atletismo. Desde hace un año soy miembro del equipo de baloncesto de mi instituto. Somos campeones regionales. Nos entrenamos dos veces a la semana en el instituto. También me gusta el fútbol. Voy a ver los partidos de mi equipo provincial en el estadio del pueblo con mis amigos. Lo pasamos muy bien. ¿Eres deportivo?

En mi tiempo libre me gusta escuchar música. Me encanta el rock, especialmente el heavy metal. Mi grupo preferido es Metálica, son fantásticos. ¿Qué tipo de música te gusta?

No me gusta ver la televisión, es aburrido. Prefiero ir al cine. Voy todas las semanas. Me gustan las películas de acción. La semana pasada fui a ver Chain Reaction con Keanu Reeves que es mi actor preferido. Me gustó mucho, es una película muy inteligente. ¿Vas a menudo al cine?

¿Qué haces en tu tiempo libre? ¿Cómo es un fin de semana típico para ti?

|   |   | Cierto | Falso |
|---|---|---|---|
| 1 | Gabriel pertenece a un equipo de baloncesto. | ☐ | ☐ |
| 2 | Su equipo se entrena en el estadio del pueblo. | ☐ | ☐ |
| 3 | Se divierte cuando ve los partidos de fútbol. | ☐ | ☐ |
| 4 | No le gusta la música. | ☐ | ☐ |
| 5 | Prefiere la televisión al cine. | ☐ | ☐ |
| 6 | Va a menudo al cine. | ☐ | ☐ |
| 7 | Va a ver Chain Reaction este fin de semana. | ☐ | ☐ |
| 8 | Le gusta Keanu Reeves porque es inteligente. | ☐ | ☐ |

Now try to correct the statements that were false.

## Task 4 — Writing

Escribe una carta a un amigo español (60 a 80 palabras). Describe lo que haces en tu tiempo libre.

Use the letter in Task 3 as a model for your own letter. Use time marker words such as *normalmente*, *a veces* and *a menudo*. Ask questions in your letter. The examiner will be marking you on how accurately (correctly) you can communicate. Make sure you understand a question before you start to answer it. Don't ignore time markers such as *normalmente*, *pasado* or *próximo* as they will indicate whether you should use the present, past or future tenses.

## Answers

**TASK 1**

1, 5, 6, 7, 10

**TASK 3**

1 Cierto 2 Falso 3 Cierto 4 Falso 5 Falso
6 Cierto 7 Falso 8 Falso

2 Su equipo se entrena en el instituto.
4 Le encanta la música.
5 Prefiere el cine a la televisión.
7 Fue a ver Chain Reaction la semana pasada.
8 Le gustó porque es una película inteligente.

## For your own notes

..................................................  ..................................................

..................................................  ..................................................

..................................................  ..................................................

..................................................  ..................................................

..................................................  ..................................................

..................................................  ..................................................

## Checklist

**How confident do you feel about these?
Can you:**

| | Fine | Help! |
|---|---|---|
| **1** answer the questions on the Foundation Checklist on page 21? | ❏ | ❏ |

*If you've ticked the Help! box, go back to the Foundation Notes/Options and revise!*

| | Fine | Help! |
|---|---|---|
| **2** ask if an activity is available? | ❏ | ❏ |
| **3** discuss times of sessions and performances? | ❏ | ❏ |
| **4** say why you prefer to do something? | ❏ | ❏ |
| **5** ask if a play or film was good? | ❏ | ❏ |
| **6** discuss and give an opinion about a film, TV programme or activity? | ❏ | ❏ |
| **7** tell someone what a film or play was about? | ❏ | ❏ |
| **8** say what you would like to do if you had the money and the time? | ❏ | ❏ |

## In my spare time

You must be able to give opinions and reasons for your opinions at this level. Make sure you know the phrases for expressing likes and dislikes by checking the word lists on pages 92–96 before you go any further. You should also be prepared to give a simple description of the plot of a film or play. You can do it in the present tense but if you want to impress the examiner you must use the past tenses (preterite and imperfect).

To describe what you would do if you, say, won the lottery you need to use the conditional and the subjunctive. It is easiest to do this by learning set phrases by heart. Draw a diagram to describe your leisure activities.

**Notes/Options**

**1** *Only once you are really sure you are confident with the Foundation Checklist should you carry on with these Higher Notes/Options.*

| | |
|---|---|
| **2** ¿Hay una discoteca por aquí/ en tu barrio? | = Is there a disco around here/in your area? |
| ¿Se puede montar a caballo por aquí? | = Can you go horse-riding around here? |
| ¿Qué ponen en el cine esta semana? | = What's on at the cinema this week? |
| ¿Qué hay en la tele esta noche? | = What's on TV tonight? |
| ¿Es posible alquilar bicicletas? | = Is it possible to hire bicycles? |
| ¿Podemos ir de excursión? | = Can we go on a trip? |
| ¿Tienes una guía de televisión? | = Do you have a TV guide? |
| **3** ¿Cuántas sesiones hay? | = How many performances/ showings are there? |
| ¿A qué hora es la sesión de la tarde? | = What time is the afternoon/evening performance? |
| ¿Es sesión continua? | = Is it a continuous performance? |
| ¿A qué hora empieza el concierto esta tarde? | = What time does this evening's concert begin? |
| ¿A qué hora termina? | = What time does it finish? |
| **4** ¿Qué prefieres hacer? | = What do you prefer to do? |
| Prefiero ir de paseo porque hace buen tiempo. | = I prefer to go for a walk because the weather is good. |
| No quiero salir porque hay fútbol en la tele. | = I don't want to go out because there is football on TV. |
| Prefiero quedarme en casa porque estoy cansado/a. | = I prefer to stay in because I'm tired. |
| **5** ¿Qué te pareció la película? | = What did you think of the film? |
| ¿Era bueno el concierto? | = Was the concert good? |
| ¿Te gustó el programa? | = Did you like the programme? |
| ¿Qué tal el teatro? | = How was the theatre? |

## Checklist

How confident do you feel about these?
Can you:

|  |  | Fine | Help! |
|---|---|---|---|
| 1 | describe your home town and local area? | ❏ | ❏ |
| 2 | say what there is to do there, including festivals? | ❏ | ❏ |
| 3 | give simple information and opinions about where you live? | ❏ | ❏ |
| 4 | ask where a place is? | ❏ | ❏ |
| 5 | say how to get to a place? | ❏ | ❏ |
| 6 | understand directions given to you? | ❏ | ❏ |
| 7 | give and understand information about using public transport? | ❏ | ❏ |
| 8 | understand simple transport signs and notices? | ❏ | ❏ |
| 9 | buy tickets for use on public transport? | ❏ | ❏ |
| 10 | buy fuel for a car and ask the cost? | ❏ | ❏ |
| 11 | ask for the tyres, water and oil to be checked? | ❏ | ❏ |
| 12 | understand and describe weather conditions? | ❏ | ❏ |

## My neighbourhood

This topic can be fun to learn because it's about your town, city, village or area. See the word lists on pages 104 and 105.

### HELP IS AT HAND!

|  | | Notes/Options |
|---|---|---|
| 1 | tu pueblo | = your town/village |
|  | ciudad | = city |
|  | barrio | = neighbourhood |
|  | Es industrial y ruidoso/a. | ruidoso/a = noisy |
|  | Es grande y moderno/a. | |
|  | Es pequeño/a y tranquilo/a. | |
|  | Es histórico/a y turístico/a. | |

### DO YOU REMEMBER THESE?

Pueblo and barrio are masculine, while ciudad is feminine:

Vivo en una ciudad ruidosa.

but

Mi barrio es muy ruidoso.

| | |
|---|---|
| ¿Dónde está tu barrio? | = Where is your area? |
| Está al norte/sur/este/oeste de Inglaterra. | = It's in the north/south/east/west of England. |
| Está en el noroeste. | noroeste = north west |
| Está a cien kilómetros de Swansea. | = It's 100 kilometres from Swansea. |
| Está en el campo. | = It's in the country. |
| Está en la costa. | = It's on the coast. |
| Tiene veinte mil habitantes. | = It has a population of 20,000. |

**2** ¿Qué hay de interés en tu ciudad para jóvenes? = What is there for young people in your city?

... para turistas? = ... for tourists?

una piscina
un estadio
pistas de tenis
un campo de fútbol
grandes almacenes
muchas tiendas
centros comerciales
un mercado
un parque zoológico
un museo
un castillo
una catedral
un teatro

¿Qué se puede hacer en tu pueblo? = What can you do in your town?

se puede { ir de compras / hacer deporte / ir de excursión

*Be prepared to talk about festivals and carnivals in your town.*

| | |
|---|---|
| Hay un carnaval en verano. | = There is a carnival in the summer. |
| Hay teatro callejero. | = There is street entertainment. |
| Hay concursos. | = There are competitions. |

**3** ¿Qué piensas de tu pueblo/ ciudad? = What do you think about your town?

| Me gusta porque | hay mucho que hacer. es muy animado/a. tiene buen ambiente. aquí viven mis amigos. |
|---|---|
| No me gusta porque | no hay nada que hacer. es muy aburrido/a. está contaminado/a. es feo/a y sucio/a. |

**4** Perdone, señor. = Excuse me.

¿Dónde está el ayuntamiento, por favor? = Where is the town hall, please?

¿Por dónde se va a la oficina de turismo? = How do you get to the tourist office?

¿Hay una farmacia por aquí? = Is there a chemist's around here?

**5/6**

Have a look at the word list on page 104 about finding places in and around a town.

Suba la calle. = Go up the street.

Baje la calle. = Go down the street.

Cruce el puente. = Cross the bridge.

Siga todo recto/derecho. = Go straight on.

Tuerza a la derecha. = Turn right.

Tuerza a la izquierda. = Turn left.

Tome la primera/segunda/ tercera a la izquierda. = Take the first/ second/third on the left.

¿Está lejos? = Is it far?

¿Está cerca? = Is it close?

Está después de los semáforos. = It's after the traffic lights.

La parada está allí. = The bus-stop is over there.

Doble la esquina. = Go round the corner.

Está al final de la calle. = It's at the end of the street.

Está fuera de la ciudad. = It's outside the city.

Está en el centro del pueblo. = It's in the centre of the town.

**7** **Por tren, autocar, autobús y metro**

Coja el autobús. = Take the bus.

Tome el metro. = Take the underground.

¿A qué hora sale el próximo tren para Madrid? = What time is the next train to Madrid?

¿Hay un autocar para Ciudad Real? = Is there a coach for Ciudad Real?

¿A qué hora llega? = What time does it arrive?

¿Cuánto tiempo dura el viaje? = How long is the journey?

Dura/tarda tres horas. = It lasts 3 hours.

¿Es directo o hay que cambiar? = Is it direct or do you have to change?

Es la próxima parada. = It's the next stop.

¿Qué línea cojo? = What line do I take?

¿Dónde está la parada de autobús? = Where is the bus-stop?

... la estación de ferrocarril/ metro? = ... the train/tube station?

**8** There are useful word lists on pages 104 and 105 of signs that you will need to recognise.

**9** **En el despacho de billetes**

Quisiera un billete para Salamanca para el día 19, con reserva de asiento. = I'd like a ticket to Salamanca for the 19th, with a reserved seat.

¿Primera o segunda clase?
En segunda.

¿Ida y vuelta? = Return?

No, sencillo. = No, one way.

¿Cuánto vale?

30,05 euros.

| | |
|---|---|
| ¿Fumador o no fumador? | = Smoking or non-smoking? |
| No fumador. | |
| Quisiera sentarme cerca de la ventanilla, si puede ser. | = I'd like to sit by the window, if possible. |
| Tome usted. Coche número 12, asiento 72, cerca de la ventanilla. | = Here you are. Carriage no. 12, seat 72, by the window. |
| Quisiera un bonobús, por favor. | = I'd like a book of bus tickets, please. |
| ¿De qué andén sale el tren a Oviedo? | = Which platform does the Oviedo train leave from? |
| ¿Es éste el andén número dos? | = Is this platform 2? |
| ¿Dónde está la vía 3? | = Where is track 3? |

## 10 En la estación de servicio

| | |
|---|---|
| ¿Gasolina o gasóleo? | = Petrol or diesel? |
| Llénelo, por favor. | = Fill it up, please. |
| ¿Me da 25 litros de sin plomo? | = Can you give me 25 litres of lead-free? |
| Póngame 30 litros de gasóleo. | = Put in 30 litres of diesel. |

## 11 ¿Algo más?

| | |
|---|---|
| ¿Puede comprobar el aceite? | = Can you check the oil? |
| Compruebe los neumáticos, por favor. | = Check the tyres, please. |
| Mire el agua, por favor. | = Check the water, please. |
| ¿Tiene un plano de carreteras? | = Do you have a road map? |
| ¿Hay servicios aquí? | = Are there toilets here? |
| ¿Vende refrescos? | = Do you sell drinks? |
| ¿Es ésta la carretera de Burgos? | = Is this the right road to Burgos? |
| la autopista | = the motorway |

## 12 El tiempo

Use the word list on page 103 for phrases about the weather.

## Going for a C?

Learn the extra vocabulary below to help you understand weather forecasts.

| | |
|---|---|
| el pronóstico la previsión | = forecast |
| nieblas/brumas matinales | = morning mist |
| vientos flojos | = breezes |
| vientos de componente este | = easterly winds |
| sin cambio en temperaturas | = no change in temperature |
| cielo cubierto | = cloudy |
| cielo claro/despejado | = clear sky |
| aumento de nubosidad | = increase in cloud cover |
| cielos con intervalos nubosos | = sunny intervals |
| alguna llovizna | = some showers |
| chubascos | = blustery showers |
| un empeoramiento | = worsening |
| un mejoramiento | = an improvement |
| inestable | = unstable |

## Test yourself

**Task 1**                     Listening

Listen to the CD (Chapter 6, Foundation). Play the track twice.
Listen to the following station announcements.

Pon una marca en las casillas correctas.

1   El tren sale a las
   a   3h 30   ☐
   b   13h 30   ☐
   c   13h 20   ☐

2   El tren llega al andén número
   a   5   ☐
   b   15   ☐
   c   25   ☐

3   El tren llega a las
   a   2h 40   ☐
   b   12h 14   ☐
   c   20h 04   ☐

4   El tren sale de la vía
   a   7   ☐
   b   17   ☐
   c   6   ☐

## Task 2 — Speaking

You are in a service-station in Spain. Use the prompts to ask for what you want.

**1** Buenos días, ¿Qué desea?

**2** Muy bien.

**3** En seguida, señor(ita).

**4** Hay que seguir todo recto.

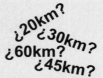

**5** Está a 50 kilómetros de aquí.

Sí, están allí, a la derecha de la caja.

**¡Ojo!** (Watch out!) You may be marked down if you use the 'tú' form of the verbs rather than the 'usted'.

## Task 3 — Reading

Empareja los dibujos con las frases.

**1** La sala de espera

  a

**2** La consigna

b

**3** El cambio de moneda

c

**4** Caballeros

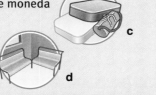  d

## Task 4 — Writing

Escribe una carta a tu corresponsal español(a). Describe tu pueblo (80 palabras).

Use this formula to help you.

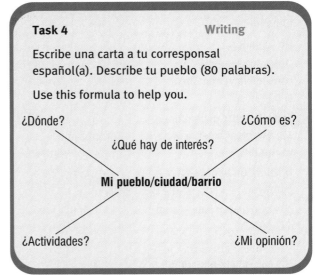

¿Dónde?                    ¿Cómo es?

¿Qué hay de interés?

**Mi pueblo/ciudad/barrio**

¿Actividades?              ¿Mi opinión?

## Answers

## Take a break

**Remember to look back at the Checklist on page 45!**

| | |
|---|---|
| Le traigo un cuchillo limpio. | = I'll bring you a clean knife. |
| Tráiganos otro tenedor. | = Bring us another fork. |
| Voy a traerles otro. | = I'll bring you another. |
| Tráigame … | = Bring me … |
| No hay mostaza. | = There is no mustard. |
| ¿Hay libro de reclamaciones? | = Is there a complaints book? |
| Tengo una queja. | = I have a complaint. |

*See also Foundation Checklist 12 and 13.*

## Going for an A?

Make sure that you can talk about your food preferences. You should also be able to understand other people's opinions about food and drink. Be prepared to talk about a recent visit you have made to a restaurant either here or abroad.

Food and drink could come up in conversations about daily routine, and health and fitness. Check Chapters 2 and 3.

## Test yourself

### Task 1       Listening

Listen to the CD twice (Chapter 8, Higher).

Llamas por teléfono a un restaurante, El Río de la Plata, en Málaga. He aquí la conversación. Contesta 'sí' o 'no' a las preguntas en tu cuestionario:

| | FRASES | SÍ o NO |
|---|---|---|
| 1 | El restaurante está abierto a la una. | |
| 2 | Está abierto tres veces al día. | |
| 3 | Está cerrado los lunes todo el año. | |
| 4 | Tiene más de un menú turístico. | |
| 5 | Todos los menús tienen el mismo precio. | |
| 6 | Los padres son vegetarianos. | |
| 7 | El camarero no sabe que el jamón es carne. | |
| 8 | Los vegetarianos tienen dos posibilidades para el primer plato. | |
| 9 | No hay más de una clase de tortilla. | |
| 10 | El restaurante está situado bastante lejos de donde se aloja la familia. | |

[10]

## Test yourself

### Task 2       Speaking

You are with your friend at a restaurant in Spain. You need to order something to eat and drink for yourself and your friend and find out what there is for dessert. Your friend doesn't eat meat. Here is the menu. Use the prompts to order your meal.

---

### ❖ MENÚ DEL DÍA ❖

| | | |
|---|---|---|
| **1° plato:** | Sopa de tomate | |
| | Gazpacho andaluz | |
| | | |
| **2° plato:** | Pescado | – bacalao |
| | Carne | – pollo asado |
| | Huevos | – tortilla española |
| | | |
| **Postres:** | Varios | |

---

¿Sí señor/señorita?

No queda tortilla. El pollo está muy bueno.

¿Y para beber?

Muy bien.

Hay flan y helado.

### Task 3       Writing

Last year you stayed at the house of your Spanish friend Sebastián. It was his birthday while you were there. Write an account of what you did on his birthday. The notes and pictures below give an outline of events.

¿Qué hiciste?

¿Qué dijiste?

¡Feliz cumpleaños!

¿A dónde llamaste?

¿Por qué?

¿A qué hora llegasteis al restaurante?

¿Dónde os sentasteis?

¿Qué pediste de primer plato? ¿Y tu compañero?

¿Y de segundo?

¿Y para beber?

¿Llegó a tiempo el primer plato?

¿Qué dijiste al camarero?

¿Qué contestó?

¿Te gustó la comida?

¿Pedisteis postre?

¿Café?

¿La cuenta?

¿La propina?

¿Cómo volvisteis a casa?

Give a clear progression through the events, using the past tenses. Add extra details if you can. Use the '-mos' ending on the verb to describe what you both did or had.

## Answers

**TASK 1**
1 no; 2 no; 3 no; 4 sí; 5 no; 6 no; 7 sí; 8 sí; 9 no; 10 no

**TASK 2** (Suggested Answers)

You  De primero, una sopa de tomate para mí y para mi amiga gazpacho andaluz. De segundo, bacalao y tortilla española.

You  Mi amiga no come carne. El bacalao entonces.

You  Tráiganos un agua mineral y un jugo de naranja.

You  ¿Qué hay de postre?

## Take a break

¡Enhorabuena! You have completed the chapter.

## Checklist

**How confident do you feel about these? Can you:**

|  |  | Fine | Help! |
|---|---|---|---|
| 1 | give details about your school: its size, type, number of pupils and facilities? | ❏ | ❏ |
| 2 | ask and talk about school routine: timetables, homework, breaks and games? | ❏ | ❏ |
| 3 | say how you travel to and from school? | ❏ | ❏ |
| 4 | say what subjects you like and why? | ❏ | ❏ |
| 5 | say what clubs and teams you belong to? | ❏ | ❏ |
| 6 | give simple opinions about your school? | ❏ | ❏ |
| 7 | say if you intend to leave or stay on at school? | ❏ | ❏ |

## At school

This topic is about you. Be prepared to talk and write about your school life in detail. Look at the word lists on pages 112–113 and make spider diagrams using the notes below to help you.

### HELP IS AT HAND!

**Notes/Options**

1 ¿Cómo se llama tu colegio/ instituto?

Mi instituto se llama ...
el instituto = secondary school

¿Cómo es tu colegio?
el colegio = high school or private school

la escuela = primary school

Es mixto. = It's mixed.
... femenino = for girls
... masculino = for boys
... católico = Catholic

¿Cómo son los edificios? edificios = buildings
Son viejos.
... modernos.

*Make a mental note that clase = lesson, and aula = classroom.*

| Hay aulas (de lenguas, de inglés, etc.) | = There are classrooms (languages, English, etc.) |
|---|---|
| ... laboratorios | = ... labs |
| ... laboratorio de lenguas | = ... language lab |
| ... campos de deportes | = ... sports grounds |
| ... canchas de tenis | = ... tennis courts |
| ... un gimnasio | = ... gym |
| ... un centro deportivo/ polideportivo | = ... sports centre |
| ... patios | = ... playgrounds |
| ... biblioteca | = ... library |
| ... cantina | = ... canteen |
| ... el despacho del director/ de la directora | = ... the headmaster's/ mistress's office |
| ... la secretaría | = ... the secretary's office |
| ... pasillos | = ... corridors |
| ... una sala de actos | = ... hall |

¿Cuántos alumnos hay? = How many pupils are there?

2 ¿En qué curso estás?

Estoy en cuarto. = I'm in the 4th year.
... quinto. = ... 5th year.
... sexto. = ... 6th year.

¿Cómo es tu horario? = What is your timetable like?

¿Qué asignaturas tienes el lunes por la mañana? = What subjects do you have on a Monday morning?

Los lunes tengo matemáticas de 9h 5 a 10h 20.

Después es el recreo. = Then it's break.

A las once menos veinte tengo ciencias. = At 10.40 I have science.

Antes de comer tengo educación física. = Before lunch I have P.E.

Use the word list on page 112 to revise school subjects.

¿A qué hora empieza el colegio? = What time does school start?

¿A qué hora empiezan las clases? = What time do lessons start?

Las clases empiezan a las 9h.

¿A qué hora termina el colegio? = What time does school finish?

¿Cuánto tiempo duran las clases? = How long do lessons last?

Duran 35 minutos.

¿A qué hora es el recreo? el recreo = break

¿Qué haces durante el recreo?

Charlo con mis amigos/as. = I chat with my friends.

Juego al fútbol.

Como algo. = I have something to eat.

Como un bocado. = I have a snack.

¿A qué hora es la comida /el almuerzo? = What time is lunch?

¿Qué haces a mediodía? = What do you do at midday?

Paso la hora de comer en la cantina. = I spend the lunch hour in the canteen.

Traigo el almuerzo. = I bring a packed lunch.

Como la comida del colegio. = I have school dinners.

Vuelvo a casa a comer. = I go home for lunch.

¿Tienes muchos deberes? = Do you have a lot of homework?

Hago dos horas de deberes todas las tardes. = I do two hours of homework every evening.

¡Sí, tengo demasiados! = Yes, I have too much.

¿Qué deportes practicas en el instituto? = What sports do you do at school?

Juego al baloncesto y hago gimnasia.

See page 94 for other sports.

3 ¿Cómo vienes al colegio? = How do you come to school?

Vengo a pie. = I come on foot.

Voy andando. = I walk.

... en bici. = ... by bike.

... en autobús. = ... by bus.

Me trae mi padre en el coche. = My father brings me in the car.

Nunca llego tarde. = I am never late.

A veces ... = Sometimes ...

Siempre ... = Always ...

4 ¿Qué asignatura prefieres y por qué?

Prefiero las ciencias porque son útiles.

Me encanta el inglés porque es fácil.

Me gustan las matemáticas porque me gusta la profesora.

¿Qué asignatura no te gusta? ¿Por qué?

Odio la informática porque no soy fuerte en esta asignatura.

soy fuerte = I'm good at

soy flojo/a = I'm weak at

5 ¿Perteneces a algún club o equipo escolar? = Do you belong to any school club or team?

Sí, pertenezco al club de teatro. = Yes, I belong to the theatre club.

Pertenezco al equipo de fútbol. = I belong to the football team.

6 ¿Qué piensas de tu instituto?

Las clases son interesantes.

Las clases son aburridas.

Aprendo mucho. = I learn a lot.

No aprendo nada.

Los profesores son simpáticos.

7 ¿Qué vas a hacer después de los exámenes? = What are you going to do after the exams?

¿Vas a dejar el colegio? = Are you going to leave school?

¿Vas a dejar los estudios?

Me quedaré en el instituto para aprobar mis 'A' levels. = I'm going to stay at school to get my 'A' levels.

Dejaré de estudiar. = I'll stop studying.

Depende de los resultados.

Voy a buscar trabajo. = I'm going to look for a job.

Voy a hacer un curso de formación profesional. = I'm going to do a training course.

... un curso de informática. = ... a computer course.

... un aprendizaje. = ... an apprenticeship.

No he decidido todavía. = I haven't decided yet.

Depende de si apruebo los exámenes. = It depends on my exam results.

Make sure you can say what your future plans are. Look at the word list on page 114 for ideas.

**2** ¿Cómo vas a trabajar? = How do you go to work?

*See Chapter 6, Foundation Notes/Options 7.*

El viaje dura tres cuartos de hora. = The journey takes 45 minutes ($\frac{3}{4}$ of an hour).

**3** ¿Trabaja tu padre/madre/ hermano/hermana? = Does your father/ mother/brother/sister work?

Sí, es ...

No, está en paro. = He/She is unemployed.

Está parado/a.

**4** *Useful phrases which you need to understand:*

| | |
|---|---|
| Las horas de trabajo son de 9h a 5h. | = The working hours are from 9 to 5 o'clock. |
| el día laborable | = the working day |
| Se necesita: Funcionario | = Wanted: Administrator |
| Se requiere: Director | = Wanted: Manager |
| Se pide: Jefe de Obras | = Wanted: Site Manager |
| Precisa: Consultores | = Wanted: Consultants |
| Solicita: Técnico | = Wanted: Technician |
| Se ofrece salario a convenir | = Salary negotiable |
| Se valora experiencia mínima | = Minimal experience appreciated |
| Requisitos | = requirements |
| Funciones | = duties |
| Formación | = training |
| Los interesados deben enviar su CV actualizado. | = Candidates should send a current CV |
| salario/sueldo | = salary |

## Work experience

| | |
|---|---|
| hacer prácticas laborales/ profesionales | = to do work experience |
| Hice mis prácticas laborales en + name of firm/ organisation. | = I did my work experience at … |
| Hice dos semanas de prácticas laborales. | = I did two weeks of work experience. |
| Tenía que archivar. | = I had to do filing. |
| … contestar el teléfono. | = … answer the phone. |
| … trabajar en una obra de construcción. | = … work on a building site. |

**5** ¿Trabajas? = Do you work?

¿Tienes un trabajo/empleo? = Do you have a job?

| | |
|---|---|
| Sí, trabajo en un supermercado. | = Yes, I work in a supermarket. |
| … en una tienda. | = … in a shop. |
| … en una hamburguesería. | = … in a hamburger restaurant. |
| … en una peluquería. | = … in a hairdresser's. |
| Reparto periódicos. | = I have a paper round. |
| Hago de canguro. | = I do baby-sitting. |
| No, no trabajo. | = No, I don't work. |

Trabajo los sábados. = I work on Saturdays.

... todas las tardes. = ... every evening.

... dos tardes a la semana. = ... two evenings a week.

¿Está bien pagado? = Is it well paid?

No está mal. Recibo siete libras y veinticinco peniques por hora. = Not bad. I get £7.25 an hour.

... cuarenta libras al día. = ... £40 a day.

No, está mal pagado. = It's badly paid.

Paga mal. = It pays badly.

*See Chapter 3, Foundation Notes/Options 11 for useful phrases to describe what you spend your money on.*

**6**  ¿Qué piensas de tu trabajo?   | What do you think of your job?

> Es interesante.
> Es aburrido.
>
> Me gusta trabajar con el público. = I like to work with people.
> Me cansa. = I get tired.
>
> Es variado.
> Es repetitivo.
>
> Mis compañeros son simpáticos.
> No me llevo bien con mis compañeros. = I don't get on with my workmates.

**7**  Look at the word lists on pages 114–115.

**8**  la publicidad   | = advertising

| | |
|---|---|
| en mi opinión … | = in my opinion … |
| el anuncio | = advert |
| la cartelera | = bill board |
| el póster | = poster |
| Los anuncios en la tele son muy entretenidos. | = TV ads. are very entertaining. |
| No los tomo en serio. | = I don't take them seriously. |
| Tienen mucha imaginación. | = They are very imaginative. |
| No representan la realidad. | = They don't represent real life. |
| Mucha gente los toma en serio. | = Lots of people take them seriously. |
| Influyen demasiado a la gente. | = They influence people too much. |

**9/10** *See Chapter 7, Foundation Notes/Options 19 for how to give and ask for a phone number.*

| | |
|---|---|
| ¿Diga? | = Hello? |
| ¿Dígame? | |
| ¿Quieres dejar un recado/ un mensaje? | = Do you want to leave a message? |
| Sí, de parte de Marcos. | = Yes, it's Marcos. |
| ¿Puedo volver a llamar dentro de media hora? | = Can I phone back in half an hour? |
| Puede volver a llamar. | = You can ring back. |
| No cuelgue. | = Don't hang up. |
| Está comunicando. | = It's engaged. |
| Marque otra vez. | = Dial again. |

## Going for a C?

How much can you understand of this advert for training courses? Use a dictionary if you get stuck.

**Con CEAC, SÍ puedes aprender.**

**Curso de Esteticista**

**Aprendes en casa**, a tu ritmo, sin horarios ni desplazamientos.

**Tendrás un profesor al teléfono** que resolverá todas tus dudas.

**Con todo el material necesario**, para que puedas practicar desde el primer día.

**Conseguirás tu diploma CEAC** que acreditará tus conocimientos y profesionalidad.

**Con la garantía CEAC:** si al terminar el curso no estás satisfecho, te reembolsaremos el dinero abonado.

**Con una institución con 50 años de experiencia.** Más de un millón y medio de alumnos han aprendido con CEAC.

**CEAC**
*En vanguardia desde 1946*
**902 102 103**
Servicio de información 24h.

## Test yourself

**Task 1**                    Listening

Listen to the CD (Chapter 10, Foundation).

Your friend's father does not speak Spanish, so you offer to listen to the message in Spanish on his answerphone.

MENSAJE POR CONTESTADOR AUTOMÁTICO

Answer the questions in your book **in English**.

1   Where is Marcos ringing from?
2   How will he get to central London?
3   **a**  What time does the train leave London?
    **b**  What time will he arrive?
4   **a**  How does he hope to get from the station to your house?
    **b**  When will he telephone again?
5   What will he bring with him? Give details.

# Chapter 4   De vacaciones

| En el hotel | At the hotel |
|---|---|
| Quisiera ... | I would like ... |
| ... la llave. | ... the key. |
| ... la cuenta. | ... the bill. |
| ... pensión completa. | ... full board. |
| ... pensión media. | ... half board. |
| ... desayuno. | ... breakfast. |
| ... una habitación individual. | ... a single room. |
| ... una habitación doble. | ... a double room. |
| ... una habitación triple. | ... a triple room. |
| ... una habitación familiar. | ... a family room. |
| ... con baño. | ... with a bath. |
| ... con ducha. | ... with a shower. |
| ... con vista al mar. | ... with a sea view. |
| ... con cama de matrimonio. | ... with a double bed. |
| ... con dos camas individuales. | ... with twin beds. |
| ... con una cuna. | ... with a cot. |
| ... con terraza. | ... with a balcony/terrace. |

| ¿Hay ... | Is/Are there ... |
|---|---|
| ... un bar en el hotel? | ... a bar in the hotel? |
| ... un minibar en la habitación? | ... a minibar in the room? |
| ... un restaurante? | ... a restaurant? |
| ... aire acondicionado? | ... air conditioning? |
| ... teléfono? | ... a telephone? |
| ... secador? | ... a hair dryer? |
| ... salas de conferencias? | ... conference rooms? |
| ... ascensor? | ... a lift? |
| ... aparcamiento? | ... parking? |
| ... garaje? | ... a garage? |
| ... jardín? | ... a garden? |
| ... terraza? | ... a balcony/terrace? |
| ... piscina? | ... a swimming pool? |
| ... gimnasio? | ... a gym? |
| ... sauna? | ... a sauna? |
| ... parque infantil? | ... a playground? |

| ¿Se puede(n) practicar ... | Is it possible to do |
|---|---|
| ... la equitación? | ... horse riding? |
| ... la pesca? | ... fishing? |
| ... la caza? | ... hunting? |
| ... el senderismo? | ... walking? |
| ... el montañismo? | ... mountaineering? |
| ... el piragüismo? | ... canoeing? |
| ... el buzo? | ... surfing? |
| ... la vela? | ... sailing? |
| ... los deportes acuáticos? | ... water sports? |

# Chapter 4   De vacaciones

| | |
|---|---|
| Tengo un problema. | I have a problem. |
| Tengo una queja. | I have a complaint. |
| El cuarto de baño está sucio. | The bathroom is dirty. |
| Hay demasiado ruido. | There is too much noise. |
| No funciona la calefacción. | The heating doesn't work. |
| No funciona el aire acondicionado. | The air conditioning doesn't work. |
| No hay bastantes mantas. | There aren't enough blankets. |
| No hay bastantes toallas. | There aren't enough towels. |
| No hay agua caliente. | There is no hot water. |
| No hay papel higiénico. | There is no toilet paper. |
| Hay un error en la cuenta. | There is a mistake on the bill. |
| ¿Dónde está ...? | Where is ...? |
| Necesito ... | I need ... |
| He reservado ... | I have reserved ... |
| ¿Está incluido el desayuno? | Is breakfast included? |
| ¿A qué hora cierra el hotel? | What time does the hotel close? |

| **En el albergue juvenil y el camping** | **At the youth hostel and campsite** |
|---|---|
| ¿Tiene una cama libre? | Do you have a free bed? |
| Es para un chico y una chica. | It's for a boy and a girl. |
| Es para dos noches. | It's for two nights. |
| ¿Necesita ver mi ... | Do you need to see my ... |
| ... tarjeta de afiliación? | ... membership card? |
| ... carnet de identidad? | ... ID card? |
| ... pasaporte? | ... passport? |
| ¿A qué hora cierra el albergue? | What time does the hostel close? |
| ¿Hay alguna tarea que hay que hacer? | Are there any jobs to be done? |
| ¿Tengo que rellenar esta ficha? | Do I have to fill in this form? |
| Quisiera alquilar ... | I'd like to hire ... |
| ... un saco de dormir. | ... a sleeping bag. |
| ... unas sábanas. | ... some sheets. |

| | |
|---|---|
| Quisiera una parcela ... | I'd like a pitch ... |
| ... para una tienda individual. | ... for a single tent. |
| ... para una tienda familiar. | ... for a family tent. |
| ... para una caravana. | ... for a caravan. |
| ... lejos de los lavabos. | ... away from the toilets. |
| ... cerca de la playa. | ... close to the beach. |
| ... al lado del río. | ... next to the river. |
| ... a las orillas del lago. | ... by the lake. |
| ... debajo de los árboles. | ... under the trees. |
| ... en la sombra. | ... in the shade. |

# Chapter 4   De vacaciones

| ¿Hay ... | Is/Are there ... |
|---|---|
| ... botellas de gas? | ... gas cylinders? |
| ... teléfono? | ... a telephone? |
| ... buzón de correos? | ... a post box? |
| ... cambio de moneda? | ... a currency exchange? |
| ... salón social? | ... a lounge? |
| ... supermercado? | ... a supermarket? |
| ... tienda? | ... a shop? |
| ... restaurante? | ... a restaurant? |
| ... cafetería? | ... a café? |
| ... mini golf? | ... a mini golf? |
| ... parque infantil? | ... a kids' playground? |
| ... agua caliente? | ... hot water? |
| ... discoteca? | ... a disco? |
| ... socorrista? | ... a life guard? |
| ... duchas de agua caliente? | ... hot water showers? |
| ... enchufes eléctricos en los lavabos? | ... electric sockets in the washrooms? |
| ... biblioteca? | ... a library? |
| ... lavandería? | ... a launderette? |
| ... piscina? | ... a swimming pool? |
| ... peluquería? | ... a hairdresser's? |
| ... tienda de recuerdos? | ... a souvenir shop? |
| ... consulta médica? | ... a doctor's surgery? |
| ... pistas de tenis? | ... tennis courts? |
| ... café de internet? | ... an internet café? |

| ¿Dónde está(n) ... | Where is/are ... |
|---|---|
| ... el dormitorio de chicos/chicas? | ... the boys'/girls' dormitories? |
| ... los aseos? | ... the toilets? |
| ... los lavabos? | ... the washrooms? |
| ... el comedor? | ... the dining room? |

| ¿Se puede ... | Is it possible to ... |
|---|---|
| ... encender lumbres? | ... light fires? |
| ... hacer barbacoas? | ... have BBQs? |
| ... pagar con tarjeta de crédito? | ... pay by credit card? |

| ¿Se puede alquilar ... | Is it possible to hire ... |
|---|---|
| ... material de camping? | ... camping equipment? |
| ... bicicletas? | ... bikes? |
| ... motos? | ... moped? |
| ... barquitos? | ... rowing boats? |

| ¡Cuidado! Peligro de incendio. | Caution! Fire danger. |
|---|---|
| Se prohibe encender fuegos. | It is forbidden to light fires. |
| No se permiten animales en el camping. | Animals are not allowed in the campsite. |
| Se ruega a los clientes guarder silencio de las 24.00 horas a las 7.00 horas. | Silence is requested from clients between 12.00am and 7.00am. |

## Chapter 5  Mis vacaciones

| Durante las vacaciones | During the holidays |
|---|---|
| Voy ... | I go ... |
| Fui ... | I went ... |
| Iré ... | I will go ... |
| ... a España. | ... to Spain. |
| ... al extranjero. | ... abroad. |
| ... al campo. | ... to the country. |
| ... a la costa. | ... to the coast. |
| ... a la sierra/montaña. | ... to the mountains. |
| ... a la playa. | ... to the beach. |
| ... a un parque temático. | ... to a theme park. |
| ... de excursión. | ... on trips. |
| ... de paseo. | ... for walks. |
| ... de compras. | ... shopping. |
| ... a las fiestas. | ... to the festivals. |
| ... a los toros. | ... to the bull fight. |
| ... de tapas. | ... to tapas bars. |
| Me alojo/quedo ... | I stay ... |
| Me alojé ... | I stayed ... |
| Me alojaré ... | I will stay ... |
| ... en un hotel. | ... at a hotel. |
| ... en un camping. | ... at a campsite. |
| ... en un albergue juvenil. | ... at a youth hostel. |
| ... en casa de mis abuelos. | ... at my grandparents' house. |
| Hago camping. | I go camping. |
| Hice camping. | I went camping. |
| Haré camping. | I will go camping. |
| Alquilo ... | I rent ... |
| Alquilé ... | I rented ... |
| Alquilaré ... | I will rent ... |
| ... una casa. | ... a house. |
| ... un chalet. | ... a villa. |
| Tomo el sol. | I sunbathe. |
| Tomé el sol. | I sunbathed. |
| Tomaré el sol. | I will sunbathe. |
| Practico ... | I do ... |
| Practiqué ... | I did ... |
| Practicaré ... | I will do ... |
| ... deportes acuáticos. | ... water sports. |
| ... la vela. | ... sailing. |
| ... el buzo. | ... scuba diving. |
| ... el surfing. | ... surfing. |
| Me baño ... | I swim ... |
| Me bañé ... | I swam ... |
| Me bañaré ... | I will swim ... |
| ... en el mar. | ... in the sea. |
| Veo ... | I watch ... |
| Vi ... | I watched ... |
| Veré ... | I will watch ... |
| ... fuegos artificiales. | ... fireworks. |
| Compro ... | I buy ... |
| Compré ... | I bought ... |
| Compraré ... | I will buy ... |
| ... recuerdos. | ... souvenirs. |
| ... regalos. | ... presents. |
| Visito ... | I visit ... |
| Visité ... | I visited ... |
| Visitaré ... | I will visit ... |
| ... a mi familia. | ... my family. |
| ... monumentos. | ... monuments. |
| ... museos. | ... museums. |

# Chapter 6   Mi pueblo

| En la estación – avisos | At the station – signs |
|---|---|
| llegadas | arrivals |
| salidas | departures |
| entrada | entrance |
| salida | exit |
| horarios | timetables |
| despacho de billetes | ticket office |
| sala de espera | waiting room |
| cambio (de moneda) | money exchange |
| información | information |
| oficina de turismo | tourist office |
| objetos perdidos | lost property |
| consigna automática | left luggage lockers |
| señoras | ladies |
| caballeros | gents |
| aseos/servicios | toilets |
| paso subterráneo | subway |
| agua potable | drinking water |
| vía | track |
| andén | platform |
| Está prohibido atravesar las vías. | Do not trespass on the tracks. |

# Chapter 7   De compras

| La ropa | Clothes |
|---|---|
| unos pantalones | trousers |
| unos pantalones cortos | shorts |
| unos vaqueros | jeans |
| una camiseta | T-shirt |
| una camisa | shirt |
| una blusa | blouse |
| un top | top |
| una falda | skirt |
| un vestido | dress |
| una chaqueta | jacket |
| un abrigo | coat |
| un impermeable | mac |
| un anorak | anorak |
| un traje | suit |
| un chándal | track suit |
| una sudadera | sweat shirt |
| una gorra | baseball cap |
| un gorro | cap/hat |
| un sombrero | hat |
| unos/un par de calcetines | (a pair of) socks |
| un panti | tights |
| un bañador | swimsuit |
| un cinturón | belt |
| una corbata | tie |
| una bufanda | scarf |
| unos guantes | gloves |
| unos/un par de zapatos | (a pair of) shoes |
| unas zapatillas deportivas | trainers |
| unas sandalias | sandals |
| unas botas | boots |
| una bolsa | bag (small) |
| un bolso | bag (large) |
| una mochila | rucksack |
| una cesta | basket |
| una cartera | briefcase |
| un billetero | wallet |
| un monedero | purse |
| un reloj | watch |
| unos pendientes | earrings |
| una cadena | chain |
| un collar | necklace |
| una pulsera | bracelet |
| un anillo | ring |
| un teléfono móvil/portátil | mobile phone |

# Chapter 7  De compras

| Las tiendas | Shops |
|---|---|
| la droguería/perfumería | drugstore |
| champú | shampoo |
| bronceador | tanning lotion |
| maquillaje | makeup |
| gel de baño/ducha | bath/shower gel |
| jabón | soap |
| un peine | comb |
| un cepillo | brush |
| un cepillo de dientes | tooth brush |
| pasta de dientes | tooth paste |
| desodorante | deodorant |
| | |
| la farmacia | chemist's/pharmacy |
| un paquete de aspirinas | packet of aspirin |
| un tubo de crema anticéptica | tube of antiseptic cream |
| crema para picaduras | cream for bites |
| loción para quemaduras | lotion for burns |
| tiritas | plasters |
| pastillas para el dolor de estómago | tablets for stomach ache |
| | |
| la tienda de comestibles/ultramarinos | grocer's |
| un paquete de té/café | packet of tea/coffee |
| un litro de agua mineral | litre of mineral water |
| un cartón de leche | carton of milk |
| un kilo de arroz | kilo of rice |
| medio kilo de queso | half a kilo of cheese |
| cuarto kilo de jamón | quarter kilo of ham |
| 200 gramos de chorizo | 200 grams of spicy sausage |
| una lata de sardinas/atún/aceitunas | tin of sardines/tuna/olives |
| una docena/media docena de huevos | dozen/half a dozen eggs |
| una botella de aceite | bottle of oil |
| un paquete de patatas fritas | packet of crisps |
| una botella de vino blanco/tinto/rosado | bottle of white/red/rosé wine |
| cerveza | beer |
| detergente | detergent |
| | |
| la frutería | fruit shop |
| unas fresas | strawberries |
| unos plátanos | bananas |
| unas manzanas | apples |
| unas peras | pears |
| un melón | melon |
| una sandía | watermelon |
| unos melocotones | peaches |
| unos albaricoques | apricots |
| unas cerezas | cherries |
| unas naranjas | oranges |
| unos limones | lemons |
| | |
| la verdulería | greengrocer's/vegetable shop |
| unas patatas | potatoes |
| una lechuga | a lettuce |
| unos tomates | tomatoes |
| unas zanahorias | carrots |
| unas cebollas | onions |
| un ajo | garlic |
| unas judías (verdes) | (green) beans |
| unos guisantes | peas |
| una berenjena | aubergine |
| un pimiento | pepper |

# Chapter 7   De compras

| Las tiendas | Shops |
|---|---|
| la carnicería | butcher's |
| unas chuletas | chops |
| un pollo | chicken |
| un bistec | steak |
| cordero | lamb |
| cerdo | pork |
| salchichas | sausages |
| | |
| la pescadería | fishmonger's |
| pescado | fish |
| unas gambas | prawns/shrimp |
| unas sardinas | sardines |
| merluza | hake |
| atún | tuna |
| bacalao | cod |
| | |
| la panadería | bakery/bread shop |
| la pastelería | bakery |
| la confitería | sweet shop |
| pan | bread |
| una hogaza de pan | loaf of bread |
| una barra de pan | French loaf |
| unos panecillos | buns |
| unos bollos | sweet buns/cakes |
| una tarta | cake/tart |
| un pedazo de tarta | slice of cake |
| un pastel | cake/pastry |
| una tableta de chocolate | bar of chocolate |
| unos caramelos | sweets |
| unos bombones | chocolates |
| un chupa chup | lollipop |
| | |
| el quiosco | kiosk |
| un periódico | newspaper |
| una revista | magazine |
| un tebeo | comic |
| | |
| el estanco | tobacconist's |
| unos sellos | stamps |
| unos sobres | envelopes |
| unas postales | postcards |
| una tarjeta | card |
| una tarjeta telefónica | telephone card |
| | |
| la tienda de recuerdos/regalos | souvenir/gift shop |
| unas castañuelas | castanets |
| una muñeca | doll |
| cerámica | pottery |
| un plato | plate |
| una jarra | jug |
| un abanico | fan |
| un pañuelo | scarf/shawl |
| un sombrero | hat |

# Present Tense

| ser – to be | |
|---|---|
| soy | I am |
| eres | you are |
| es | he/she/it is/you are |
| somos | we are |
| sois | you are |
| son | they/you are |

| salir – to go out | |
|---|---|
| salgo | I go out |
| sales | you go out |
| sale | he/she/it goes out/you go out |
| salimos | we go out |
| salís | you go out |
| salen | they/you go out |

| hacer – to do, make | |
|---|---|
| hago | I do |
| haces | you do |
| hace | he/she/it does/you do |
| hacemos | we do |
| hacéis | you do |
| hacen | they/you do |

## Reflexive Verbs

| levantarse – to get up | |
|---|---|
| **me** levanto | I get up |
| **te** levantas | you get up |
| **se** levanta | he/she/it gets up/you get up |
| **nos** levantamos | we get up |
| **os** levantáis | you get up |
| **se** levantan | they/you get up |

## Radical changing Verbs

| querer – to want/wish | |
|---|---|
| quiero | I want |
| quieres | you want |
| quiere | he/she/it wants/you want |
| queremos | we want |
| queréis | you want |
| quieren | they/you want |

# Present Tense

| dormir – to sleep | |
|---|---|
| duermo | I sleep |
| duermes | you sleep |
| duerme | he/she/it sleeps/you sleep |
| dormimos | we sleep |
| dormís | you sleep |
| duermen | they/you sleep |

*Time markers*

| Todos los días | Every day |
|---|---|
| Hoy | Today |
| Ahora | Now |
| Generalmente | Generally |
| Normalmente | Normally |
| A las 7.00 | At 7 o'clock |

# Future Tense

| Pronouns | |
|---|---|
| yo | I |
| tú | you (informal, singular) |
| él/ella/usted | he/she/it/you (formal, singular) |
| nosotros | we |
| vosotros | you (informal, plural) |
| ellos/ellas/ustedes | they/you (formal, plural) |

## Regular Verbs: -ar, -er and -ir verbs (same endings added to infinitive for all three)

| ir – to go | |
|---|---|
| iré | I will go |
| irás | you will go |
| irá | he/she/it/you will go |
| iremos | we will go |
| irán | they/you will go |

## Irregular Verbs

| tener – to have | |
|---|---|
| tendré | I will have |
| tendrás | you will have |
| tendrá | he/she/it/you will have |
| tendremos | we will have |
| tendréis | you will have |
| tendrán | they/you will have |

# Future Tense

| **decir – to say** | |
| --- | --- |
| diré | I will say |
| dirás | you will say |
| dirá | he/she/it/you will say |
| diremos | we will say |
| diréis | you will say |
| dirán | they/you will say |

| **venir – to come** | |
| --- | --- |
| vendré | I will come |
| vendrás | you will come |
| vendrá | he/she/it/you will come |
| vendremos | we will come |
| vendréis | you will come |
| vendrán | they/you will come |

| **hacer – to do, make** | |
| --- | --- |
| haré | I will do |
| harás | you will do |
| hará | he/she/it/you will do |
| haremos | we will do |
| haréis | you will do |
| harán | they/you will do |

| **poder – to be able (can)** | |
| --- | --- |
| podré | I will be able |
| podrás | you will be able |
| podrá | he/she/it/you will be able |
| podremos | we will be able |
| podréis | you will be able |
| podrán | they/you will be able |

| **poner – to put** | |
| --- | --- |
| pondré | I will put |
| pondrás | you will put |
| pondrá | he/she/it/you will put |
| pondremos | we will put |
| pondréis | you will put |
| pondrán | they/you will put |

# Future Tense

| | |
|---|---|
| **salir – to go out** | |
| saldré | I will go out |
| saldrás | you will go out |
| saldrá | he/she/it/you will go out |
| saldremos | we will go out |
| saldréis | you will go out |
| saldrán | they/you will go out |

| | |
|---|---|
| **haber – to have** | |
| habré | I will have |
| habrás | you will have |
| habrá | he/she/it/you will have |
| habremos | we will have |
| habréis | you will have |
| habrán | they/you will have |

| | |
|---|---|
| **saber – to know** | |
| sabré | I will know |
| sabrás | you will know |
| sabrá | he/she/it/you will know |
| sabremos | we will know |
| sabréis | you will know |
| sabrán | they/you will know |

| | |
|---|---|
| **querer – to want, wish** | |
| querré | I will want/wish |
| querrás | you will want/wish |
| querrá | he/she/it/you will want/wish |
| querremos | we will want/wish |
| querréis | you will want/wish |
| querrán | they/you will want/wish |

# Immediate Future: ir + a + infinitive

| | |
|---|---|
| **salir – to go out** | |
| voy a salir | I am going to go out |
| vas a salir | you are going to go out |
| va a salir | he/she/it/you are going to go out |
| vamos a salir | we are going to go out |
| vais a salir | you are going to go out |
| van a salir | they/you are going to go out |

# Future Tense

*Time markers*

| | |
|---|---|
| Esta tarde | This afternoon/evening |
| Mañana | Tomorrow |
| Mañana por la mañana | Tomorrow morning |
| Este fin de semana | This weekend |
| El domingo que viene | Next Sunday |
| La semana que viene | Next week |
| El año que viene | Next year |
| En el futuro | In the future |
| Al terminar mis estudios | When I finish my studies |

## Before you start

The following mock exam is based on the requirements of a variety of exam boards – all aiming for the same standards. So if you do well in this mock, you should do well in your exam.

## The four skills

### Listening

Make sure you have a clock and paper to jot ideas on. Have the CD ready. Take five minutes to read the questions before starting the CD. Answer all the questions in the spaces provided. Write neatly and put down all the information. The marks are shown by each question. Allow yourself 30 minutes if you are doing the Foundation/Higher Level, or 40 minutes if you are doing the Higher.

### Speaking

Use ten minutes' preparation time to prepare your role plays. Allow two minutes for the role plays – extra time is allowed for using the cassette recorder. You should have a blank cassette in another recorder to enable you to record your answers, and therefore mark yourself more accurately. If this is not possible, ask a friend to mark you or mark yourself after each question so that you don't forget what you have said. Remember to give opinions and reasons at every opportunity. Make sure you can show that you know how to use the past and future tenses as well as present. In the Conversation section (not included in this mock exam practice) of the Speaking paper try to sound as spontaneous as possible. If you rely on the examiner to prompt you with questions you might get asked a question you don't understand! Let the conversation flow, don't just answer the questions – add comments and detail.

### Reading

Don't spend too much time on each question – you might run out of time for other questions. You can always go back to a question when you've done the rest of the paper. Allow yourself 40 minutes if you are doing Foundation, and 1 hour for Higher – remember to answer all the questions and to write neatly!

### Writing

Allow yourself 50 minutes for Foundation, and 1 hour for Higher.

## Listening: Foundation
### Exercise 1  En casa de tu(s) amiga/o(s)
¿Qué quiere?

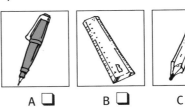

A ☐    B ☐    C ☐    D ☐

[1]

### Exercise 2
¿Qué deporte prefiere?

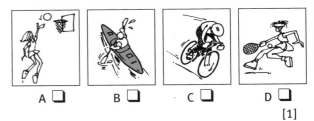

A ☐    B ☐    C ☐    D ☐

[1]

### Exercise 3
¿Dónde está el jersey?

A ☐    B ☐    C ☐    D ☐

[1]

### Exercise 4  En el centro
¿Dónde está la oficina de turismo?

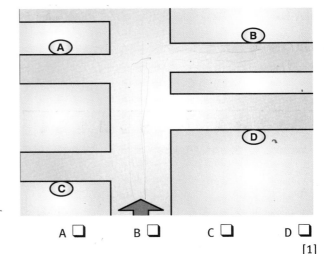

A ☐    B ☐    C ☐    D ☐

[1]

## Exercise 5  En unos grandes almacenes

¿Dónde están las camisetas?

|  | PLANTA BAJA | 1a PLANTA | 3a PLANTA | 5a PLANTA |  |
|---|---|---|---|---|---|
|  | A ☐ | B ☐ | C ☐ | D ☐ | [1] |

## Exercise 6  En la estación

¿A qué hora sale el tren?

|  | 10.00 | 12.00 | 20.00 | 02.00 |  |
|---|---|---|---|---|---|
|  | A ☐ | B ☐ | C ☐ | D ☐ | [1] |

## Exercise 7  Transportes

¿Cómo va Elena al colegio?

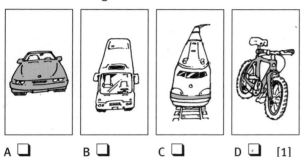

A ☐       B ☐       C ☐       D ☑   [1]

## Exercise 8  Planes para mañana

¿Adónde van a ir?

A ☐       B ☐       C ☐       D ☐   [1]

## Exercise 9  La familia

Rellena los espacios en esta ficha personal.          [4]

### F I C H A   P E R S O N A L

| Apellidos | Amestoy Fernández |
|---|---|
| Nombre(s) | Pilar |
| Edad | 16 |
| Nacida el | 2 de _____ de 1982 |
| Hermanos (número) | 3 |

| Nombre(s) | Edad | Profesión |
|---|---|---|
| Miguel | _____ | mecánico |
| Enrique | 21 | _____ |
| _____ | 25 | enfermera |

## Exercise 10  El colegio

Rellena los espacios en este horario.          [4]

| Hora | LUNES | MARTES |
|---|---|---|
| 09.00 |  | Lengua |
| 10.00 | Música | Historia |
| 11.00 |  |  |
| 11.15 | Matemáticas | Geografía |
| 12.15 | Dibujo |  |
| 1.15 | Comida |  |
| 3.30 | Informática | Literatura |
|  | Lengua | Deportes |

# Listening: Foundation/Higher

## Exercise 11  La visita de Carlos

¿Qué vais a hacer?

A   El lunes ........................................................

B   El martes ....................................................

C   El miércoles ..............................................   [3]

## Exercise 12  David Bowie

Completa los detalles.

David Bowie va a visitar Madrid y Barcelona en el

mes de ...........................................................

y puede sacarlas desde ...........................................   [2]

## Exercise 13  Vitoria

Your mother mistakenly thinks Vitoria is a person. You explain it is a town in Spain and answer her questions about it.

A   In which part of Spain is Vitoria?

.................................................................................

B   Which is the most important industry?

.................................................................................

C   What is Vitoria like?

.................................................................................

D   In which month are the main festivals?

.................................................................................   [4]

127

## Listening: Higher

### Exercise 14   El carácter

Pon una X en la casilla correcta.

1   A  ☐   Pablo es una persona ambiciosa.
    B  ☑   Pablo es una persona que quiere divertirse mucho.
    C  ☐   Pablo es una persona sensible.
    D  ☐   Pablo es una persona valiente.

2   A  ☑   Inma es una persona ambiciosa.
    B  ☐   Inma es una persona que quiere divertirse mucho.
    C  ☐   Inma es una persona sensible.
    D  ☐   Inma es una persona valiente.

3   A  ☐   Carmen es una persona ambiciosa.
    B  ☐   Carmen es una persona que quiere divertirse mucho.
    C  ☑   Carmen es una persona sensible.
    D  ☑   Carmen es una persona valiente.   [3]

### Exercise 15   Un accidente

Completa los detalles.

Muertos   ...................................................

Hora   ...................................................

Lugar   ...................................................

¿Qué pasó?   ...................................   [4]

### Exercise 16   El turismo

Explica lo que es el 'turismo diesel'.

...................................................   [1]

### Exercise 17   En una cafetería

Pon una X en la casilla correcta.   [3]

1   ¿De qué se trata esta conversación?
    A  ☐   El ocio
    B  ☑   La moda
    C  ☐   El turismo
    D  ☐   La compra

2   ¿Cómo describirías a Carlos?
    A  ☐   Valiente
    B  ☐   Extrovertido
    C  ☐   Ambicioso
    D  ☐   Tímido

3   ¿Y a su amigo?
    A  ☐   Abierto
    B  ☐   Moderno
    C  ☐   Tolerante
    D  ☐   No muy atrevido

### Exercise 18   El tiempo

Estás de vacaciones en Motril, en la Costa del Sol. Escuchas los pronósticos del tiempo.

Pon una X en la casilla que corresponde a lo que vas a hacer.

A ☐                 B ☐                 C ☐     [1]

Explica tu decisión:

...................................................   [2]

### Exercise 19   Un empleo

¿Cuáles son las ventajas de este empleo?

...................................................
...................................................   [2]

### Exercise 20   La vida sana

¿Por qué es sana la vida de este señor?  Escribe dos cosas.

...................................................
...................................................   [2]

### Exercise 21   Un recado

Te quedas en casa de tu amiga española. Cuando vuelves a casa hay un recado en el contestador automático. ¿Dónde está la discoteca? Escribe tres detalles.

...................................................
...................................................
...................................................   [3]

### Exercise 22   Los intereses

Pon una X en la casilla correcta.   [3]

1   A  ☐   Elena parece una persona seria.
    B  ☐   Elena parece una persona ligera.
    C  ☐   Elena parece una persona con intereses científicos.
    D  ☐   Elena parece una persona con intereses deportivos.

## 6 Formation: Reflexive Verbs

Reflexive verbs have object pronouns before the different parts of the verb.

| BAÑARSE = to bathe, have a bath | |
|---|---|
| *present* | *preterite* |
| me baño | me bañé |
| te bañas | te bañaste |
| se baña | se bañó |
| nos bañamos | nos bañamos |
| os bañáis | os bañasteis |
| se bañan | se bañaron |

More verbs that follow this pattern:

| acostarse | = to go to bed |
|---|---|
| dormirse | = to go to sleep |
| ducharse | = to have a shower |
| lavarse | = to (have a) wash |
| levantarse | = to get up |
| llamarse | = to be called |
| pasearse | = to go for a walk |
| tumbarse | = to lie down |

Ponerse is an irregular reflexive verb:

| PONERSE = to put on clothes | |
|---|---|
| *present* | *preterite* |
| me pongo | me puse |
| te pones | te pusiste |
| se pone | se puso |
| nos ponemos | nos pusimos |
| os ponéis | os pusisteis |
| se ponen | se pusieron |

Here is a radical-changing reflexive verb:

| HERIRSE = to hurt oneself | |
|---|---|
| *present* | *preterite* |
| me hiero | me herí |
| te hieres | te heriste |
| se hiere | se hirió |
| nos herimos | nos herimos |
| os herís | os heristeis |
| se hieren | se hirieron |

| CONOCERSE = to know each other |
|---|
| ¿Os conocéis? = Do you know each other? |
| Nos conocemos. = We know each other. |

## 7 Present Continuous Tense

To form the present continuous tense, you take the present tense of **estar** and the present participle of the verb. To form the present participle:

- **-ar** verbs: Remove the **-ar** and add **-ando**.
- **-er** and **-ir** verbs: Remove the **-er** or the **-ir** and add **-iendo**.

Here is an example in the present continuous tense:

| ESTUDIAR = to study | |
|---|---|
| estoy estudiando | I am studying |
| estás estudiando | you are studying |
| está estudiando | he/she/it/you (polite) are studying |
| estamos estudiando | we are studying |
| estáis estudiando | you are studying (plural) |
| están estudiando | they/you (polite plural) are studying |

## 8 Preterite Tense

The preterite tense is used to describe completed actions in the past:

See Regular, Irregular, Radical Changing Verbs and Reflexive (1, 2, 3 and 6 above) for examples.

Even if the action went on for a long time, if it is completed, the preterite must be used.

Fui a la escuela durante seis años. = I went to primary school for six years.

## 9 Imperfect Tense

The imperfect tense is used to describe something which was happening, or used to happen, or for descriptions in the past:

| DESAYUNAR = to have breakfast | |
|---|---|
| desayun**aba** | = I was having/used to have breakfast |
| desayun**abas** | = you were having/used to have breakfast |
| desayun**aba** | = he/she/it/you (polite) was/were having/used to have breakfast |
| desayun**ábamos** | = we were having/used to have breakfast |
| desayun**abais** | = you (plural) were having/used to have breakfast |
| desayun**aban** | = they/you (polite plural) were having/used to have breakfast |

| COMER = to eat, have lunch | |
|---|---|
| com**ía** | = I was eating/used to eat |
| com**ías** | = you were eating/used to eat |
| com**ía** | = he/she/it/you (polite) was/were eating/used to eat |
| com**íamos** | = we were eating/used to eat |
| com**íais** | = you (plural) were eating/used to eat |
| com**ían** | = they/you (polite plural) were eating/used to eat |

The **-ir** verbs have the same endings as the **-er** verbs:

viv**ía** = I was living/used to live

## 10 Perfect Tense

You use the perfect tense when you want to say that you have, or someone has, done something. You form it by using the present tense of **haber** followed by the past participle:

| HABER = to have | |
| --- | --- |
| *present* | |
| he | I have |
| has | you have |
| ha | he/she/it/you (polite) have |
| hemos | we have |
| habéis | you have (plural) |
| han | they/you (polite plural) have |

To form the past participle:

- **-ar** verbs: Remove the **-ar** from the infinitive and add **-ado**.

    dejar = to leave (deposit)  dejado

- **-er** and **-ir** verbs: Remove the **-er** and the **-ir** and add **-ido**.

    perder = to lose  perdido
    vivir = to live  vivido
    He dejado mi maleta en la consigna.  = I have left my suitcase in left luggage.

### Watch out for these irregular past participles!

| infinitive | past participle |
| --- | --- |
| abrir = to open | abierto |
| decir = to speak | dicho |
| escribir = to write | escrito |
| hacer = to do, make | hecho |
| poner = to put | puesto |
| romper = to break | roto |
| ver = to see | visto |
| volver = to want | vuelto |

## 11 Irregular Imperfects

| SER = to be | IR = to go | VER = to see |
| --- | --- | --- |
| era | iba | veía |
| eras | ibas | veías |
| era | iba | veía |
| éramos | íbamos | veíamos |
| erais | ibais | veíais |
| eran | iban | veían |

It is very important to be aware of the difference between the preterite and the imperfect tense:

- You must use the imperfect to describe something which was going on.
- You must use the preterite to describe something which came to interrupt it.

Learn these examples to use as models:

Cuando cruzaba la calle le atropelló el coche.  = She was crossing the street when she got run over by the car.

Mientras estábamos de compras nos encontramos con mi tía.  = While we were shopping we met my aunt.

## 12 Imperfect Continuous

To translate 'was … -ing', you use the imperfect continuous. It is formed by using the imperfect of **estar** with the present participle:

Estaba lloviendo.  = It was raining.

## 13 Phrases using 'Gustar'

There is no word in Spanish for 'to like'. To say that you like something or somebody, you have to say that it is pleasing to you:

Me gusta el deporte.  = I like sport.

Te gusta ir al polideportivo.  = You like going to the sports centre.

Le gusta desayunar bien.  = You (polite) He/She/It/like(s) to have a good breakfast.

Nos gusta el español.  = We like Spanish.

¿Os gusta bailar?  = Do you (plural) like dancing?

Les gustan las fiestas.  = They, you (polite plural) like the festivals.

To say that you like or someone else likes more than one thing, add an '**n**' to the end of **gusta**:

Me gustan las películas de acción.  = I like action films.

Le gustan los programas de actualidad.  = You (polite) He/She/ like(s) documentaries.

## 14 Personal 'a'

If a verb is followed by a person as the direct object, you insert an '**a**':

Juana lleva a Miguel en su coche.  = Juana takes Miguel in her car.

No conozco a Luisa.  = I don't know Luisa.

### Watch out for these exceptions!

After **tener**: Tengo tres hermanos. = I have three brothers and sisters.
When the person is not specified: Se buscan camareros. = Wanted: Waiters
When a group of people in general is referred to: Quiero oír los cantantes. = I want to hear the singers.

## 15 Pluperfect Tense

The pluperfect tense in English is translated by the imperfect in Spanish:

Estudiaba inglés desde los doce años.  = She had studied English since she was 12.

The pluperfect tense in Spanish translates as 'had done something'. It is similar to the perfect tense, except that the imperfect of **haber** is used instead of the present tense:

No le había visto. | = I had not seen him.

## 16 Future: Using 'ir a'

You can talk about what you or somebody else is going to do by using the present tense of **ir** followed by **a** and an infinitive:

Van a venir mañana. | = They are going to come tomorrow.

¿Vas a ir al cine? | = Are you going to the cinema?

## 17 Future Tense

If the verb is regular, you form the future by using the infinitive and the correct endings: -é, -ás, -á, -emos, -éis, -án.

Some verbs are irregular and do not use their infinitives:

| infinitive | future |
|---|---|
| decir = to say | diré |
| haber = to have | habré |
| hacer = to do | haré |
| poder = to be able | podré |
| querer = to want | querré |
| salir = to go out | saldré |
| tener = to have | tendré |
| venir = to come | vendré |
| El sábado visitaré a mis abuelos. | = On Saturday I will visit my grandparents. |
| ¿Qué harás en el futuro? | = What will you do in the future? |

## 18 Conditional Tense

The conditional is formed like the future tense, but with these endings:

-ía, -ías, -ía, -íamos, -íais, -ían.

Me gustaría ir a Escocia. | = I would like to go to Scotland.

Podrías venir en agosto. | = You could come in August.

## 19 Subjunctive

Use this guide to help you learn what parts of the subjunctive are relevant to your level:

- Foundation: you need to learn set phrases in the present subjunctive. E.g. ¡Que aproveche!
- Higher: you will need to recognise all forms of the subjunctive in the Listening and Reading papers.
- You will be able to get a good grade without actually using it. Use other tenses to avoid it.

- Going for an 'A'?: learn a few phrases for each topic, especially to express opinions/reasons.

### The present subjunctive

To form the present subjunctive, take the first person singular of the present tense, remove the final o and add the correct endings:

- **-ar verbs**: -e, -es, -e, -emos, -éis, -en.
- **-er and -ir verbs**: -a, -as, -a, -amos, -áis, -an.

**Watch out!**
Some verbs don't follow the rule with regard to the stem:

| infinitive | present subjunctive | |
|---|---|---|
| dar | dé | I might give. |
| estar | esté | I might be. |
| haber | haya | I might have. |
| ir | vaya | I might go. |
| saber | sepa | I might know. |
| ser | sea | I might be. |

### When is the subjunctive used?

Here are some examples:

- Imperative: all polite forms and negative familiar forms. See also note 25.
- To express a wish:

¡Ojalá gane la lotería! | = If only/I wish I could win the lottery!

¡Que aproveche! | = Enjoy your meal!

- After **quizás** or **tal vez** to express doubt:

Tal vez vaya al cine. | = Perhaps I'll go to the cinema.

- To express 'ought', 'might' and 'would like':

Quisiera un kilo de peras. | = I'd like a kilo of pears.

- In impersonal expressions:

No es posible que sea la verdad. | = It can't be true.

- In negative statements of 'saying', 'believing', etc.:

No creo que haya pasado nada. | = I don't think anything has happened.

- After **para que**:

Pon la radio para que pueda oír las noticias. | = Turn on the radio so that I can hear the news.

- After a verb of wanting or preferring that someone should do something, or that something should happen:

Quiero que salga el sol. | = I want the sun to shine.

- After a verb expressing emotion:

Siento que te hayan robado. | = I'm sorry you have been robbed.

Me alegro que vengas a verme. = I'm glad you are coming to see me.

- After a verb 'asking', 'telling', 'recommending' someone to do something:

Le ruego me mande información. = Please send me information.

- After **cuando** and **en cuanto** when followed by a future idea:

Iré a la universidad cuando termine el colegio. = I'll go to university when I finish school.

- After **sin que**:

Quiero salir del colegio sin que me vea el profesor. = I want to leave the school without being seen by the teacher.

- After **hasta que**:

Debemos quedarnos aquí hasta que deje de llover. = We should stay here until it stops raining.

Necesito ver a un médico que hable inglés. = I need to see a doctor who speaks English.

- After **antes de que**:

Te daré mi dirección antes de que te vayas. = I'll give you my address before you leave.

## 20  Verbs followed by an Infinitive

When two verbs are together, with the second one in the infinitive, sometimes it is necessary to put **a**, sometimes **de**, before the infinitive. There are some common structures using verbs which take no preposition:

| | |
|---|---|
| conseguir = to manage, get | poder = to be able to |
| deber = to have to | preferir = to prefer |
| decidir = to decide | querer = to want, wish |
| pensar = to think | |

Quiero comer. = I want to eat.
Conseguimos comerlo todo. = We managed to eat it all.

Prefieren ver la tele. = They prefer to watch TV.

- Verbs which take **a**:

| | |
|---|---|
| ayudar a = to help | ir a = to go to |
| empezar a = to start to | venir a = to come to |
| enseñar a = to show, teach | volver a = to begin again |
| invitar a = to invite | |

Vengo a verte. = I've come to see you.
Ayudamos a fregar los platos. = We help to wash up.

- Verbs which take **de**:

acabar de = to have just finished
dejar de = to stop, leave off
tener ganas de = to feel like

terminar de = to have just stopped
tratar de = to try to
Acabo de volver. = I have just got back.
Dejaré de fumar. = I will give up smoking.

## 21  Infinitives after Prepositions

In English, prepositions are often followed by the present participle of a verb. In Spanish, the infinitive is used:

| | |
|---|---|
| al pasar por la caja | = on paying at the cash desk |
| antes de desayunar | = before breakfast |
| después de casarse | = after getting married |
| sin esperarles | = without waiting for them |

## 22  Questions

In Spanish, questions start and finish with a question mark (the first is always upside down):

¿Puedo reservar un asiento? = Can I reserve a seat?

Question words have accents:

| | |
|---|---|
| ¿Dónde vives? | = Where do you live? |
| ¿Cuándo es tu cumpleaños? | = When is your birthday? |
| ¿Cómo eres? | = What are you like? |
| ¿Qué número usas? | = What is your shoe size? |
| ¿Cuál es tu color favorito? | = What is your favourite colour? |
| ¿Cuánto es? | = How much is it? |

Some of these words change to agree with plural nouns:

¿Cuáles son tus pasatiempos preferidos?

¿Quiénes son tus amigos?

These also change in order to agree with the masculine and feminine nouns that they refer to:

¿Cuántas hermanas tienes?

¿Cuántos años tienes?

**¿Por qué? and porque**

¿por qué ...? = why ...? (question)

porque ... = because ... (answer)

¿Por qué te gustan las ciencias?

Porque son interesantes.

## 23 Negatives and Affirmatives

nada = nothing

nadie = nobody

ni ... ni = neither ... nor ...

nunca/jamás = never

ninguno/a/os/as = no (adj.), none

tampoco = (n)either

When the adjective **ninguno** comes before a masculine singular noun, it loses its final o and becomes **ningún**:

| | |
|---|---|
| ningún ruido | = no noise |

When the negative word comes after the verb, **no** is placed before the verb:

| | |
|---|---|
| No viene nadie. | = Nobody is coming. |

If the negative word comes before the verb, **no** is not required:

| | |
|---|---|
| Nunca como carne. | = I never eat meat. |

To affirm a statement use: **sí, cierto, ciertamente, también**.

| | |
|---|---|
| Sí, es cierto. | = Yes, it's true. |
| Juan viene también. | = Juan is coming too. |

## 24 'Por' and 'Para'

**Por** and **para** both mean 'for'. Use **por** to mean:

- 'on behalf of':

| | |
|---|---|
| Hablé por él. | = I spoke on his behalf. |

- 'in exchange for':

| | |
|---|---|
| Pagué 20 euros por los vaqueros. | = I paid 20 euros for the jeans. |
| Gracias por la postal. | = Thanks for the postcard. |

- to denote time:

| | |
|---|---|
| Mañana por la mañana. | = Tomorrow morning. |
| Por un momento. | = For a moment. |

- 'through', 'which', 'along', 'around':

| | |
|---|---|
| Paseamos por el parque. | = We strolled through the park. |
| ¿Hay una farmacia por aquí? | = Is there a chemist's around here? |

- to denote manner or means:

| | |
|---|---|
| Hablar por teléfono. | = To speak on the telephone. |
| Conseguí el puesto por enchufe. | = I got the job through 'string pulling'. |

Use **para** for all other meanings of 'for'.

**Por** can also be used to mean 'by'.

## 25 Imperative

Imperatives are used for giving instructions and commands.

- For a positive command, take the infinitive of a verb and remove the ending. Then add the endings given below. (These only refer to the second and third persons.)

- For a negative command, take the first person singular of the present tense and remove the **o**.

When talking to friends, relations and children, use the **tú** and **vosotros/as** forms:

| | | POSITIVE | NEGATIVE |
|---|---|---|---|
| -ar (dejar) | singular | -a | -es |
| | plural | -ad | -éis |
| -er (comer) | singular | -e | -as |
| | plural | -ed | -áis |
| -ir (decidir) | singular | -e | -as |
| | plural | -id | -áis |

| *singular* | *plural* |
|---|---|
| ¡Levántate! | ¡Levantaos! = Get up! |
| ¡No te levantes! | ¡No os levantéis! = Don't get up! |
| ¡Dame! | ¡Dadme! = Give me! |
| ¡Cruza la plaza! | ¡Cruzad la plaza! = Cross the square! |

When talking to adults who are not close friends or relatives, use **usted** and **ustedes**:

| | | POSITIVE | NEGATIVE |
|---|---|---|---|
| -ar | polite singular | -e | -e |
| | polite plural | -en | -en |
| -er and -ir | polite singular | -a | -a |
| | polite plural | -an | -an |

| *singular* | *plural* |
|---|---|
| ¡Levántese! | ¡Levántense! |
| ¡No se levante! | ¡No se levanten! |
| ¡Deme! | ¡Denme! |
| ¡Cruce la plaza! | ¡Crucen la plaza! |

## 26 Exclamations!

Note the accent on the **qué** and the upside down exclamation mark at the beginning of the exclamation:

| | |
|---|---|
| ¡Qué amable! | = How kind! |
| ¡Qué bonito! | = How lovely! |
| ¡Qué asco! | = How revolting! |
| ¡Qué lástima! | = What a pity! |
| ¡Qué zapatos tan/más bonitos! | = What nice shoes! |
| ¡Cómo es posible! | = How is that possible! |
| ¡Ni hablar! | = No way! |

## 27 Passive

The passive describes the idea of an action being done to somebody or something. To form the passive, use either **ser** or **estar** followed by the past participle.

- Use **estar** to describe a state:

  El banco está cerrado.  = The bank is shut.

- Use **ser** to describe an action:

  La puerta es cerrada por el conserje.  = The door is shut by the porter.

Translate 'by' with **por**. Remember that the past participle acts like an adjective and has to agree.

### How to avoid using the passive?

- Use the reflexive form:

  Se habla español.  = Spanish is spoken.

- Change the word order, changing it from passive to active:

  Un policía le entrevistó.  = A policeman interviewed him.

- Make the verb active and use the 'they' form, which makes it sound indefinite:

  Paran los pasajeros en la aduana.  = The passengers are stopped at Customs.

# NOUNS

## 1 Gender

Nouns in Spanish are either masculine or feminine. To make nouns plural you generally add an 's'.

| MASCULINE | FEMININE | PLURAL |
|---|---|---|
| niño | niña | niños/niñas |
| mano | pierna | manos/piernas |
| bolígrafo | goma | bolígrafos/gomas |
| padre | madre | padres/madres |

All the above end in vowels. For nouns that end in a consonant add 'es' to make the plural:

| singular | plural |
|---|---|
| pez | peces |
| lápiz | lápices |
| camión | camiones |
| profesor | profesores |
| árbol | árboles |

Some words gain or lose an accent in the plural. Words ending in 'z' in the singular change the 'z' to a 'c' then add 'es' for the plural, e.g.: **lápiz, lápices**.

## 2 Definite Articles

The word for 'the' changes according to whether the noun is masculine, feminine or plural:

| MASCULINE | PLURAL | FEMININE | PLURAL |
|---|---|---|---|
| **el** hermano | **los** hermanos | **la** hermana | **las** hermanas |

**BEWARE**! There are a few exceptions where nouns ending in '-a' take **el**: el agua.

## 3 Indefinite Articles

The words for 'a', 'an' and 'some' also change:

| MASCULINE | PLURAL | FEMININE | PLURAL |
|---|---|---|---|
| un amigo | unos amigos | una amiga | unas amigas |

The pronoun **lo** is used in front of an adjective:

| lo mejor | = the best |
|---|---|
| lo peor | = the worst |
| lo importante | = the important thing |
| lo de la lotería | = the business about the lottery |

**lo que** is used to express 'that which', 'what':

No entiendo lo que dicen.  = I don't understand what they are saying.

### When can I omit the article?

- After **tener** in most negative statements:

  No tengo hermanos.  = I don't have any brothers or sisters.

- The article is omitted with nationalities and jobs:

  Mi padre es cocinero.  = My father is a cook.

### When do I keep the article in?

- With parts of the body:
  Me duele la cabeza. = I have a headache.

- With titles such as: el señor Ruiz, la señorita Dolores, la señora Borreguero.

- With school subjects:
  Me gusta el inglés.

## 4 Articles with Verbal Nouns

The structure of **el** in front of a verb can be translated as '-ing' in certain circumstances:

El fumar es malo para la salud. = Smoking is bad for your health.

# ADJECTIVES

## 1 Formation and Gender

Adjectives agree with the noun they describe so they also have masculine, feminine and plural forms. Remember you add '-s' to make the adjective plural.

| MASCULINE | PLURAL | FEMININE | PLURAL |
|---|---|---|---|
| negro | negros | negra | negras |
| guapo | guapos | guapa | guapas |
| el chico guapo | los chicos guapos | la chica guapa | las chicas guapas |

Most adjectives end in 'o' for masculine and 'a' for feminine.

### BEWARE!

Here are a few of the many exceptions:

| MASCULINE | PLURAL | FEMININE | PLURAL |
|---|---|---|---|
| inteligente | inteligentes | inteligente | inteligentes |
| grande | grandes | grande | grandes |
| azul | azules | azul | azules |
| gris | grises | gris | grises |

Adjectives of nationality ending in a consonant in their masculine singular add '-a' for the feminine singular and 'as' for the feminine plural.

| *singular* | *plural* |
|---|---|
| el chico es español | los chicos son españoles |
| la chica es española | las chicas son españolas |

> **Watch out!**
> There are some adjectives which lose the final 'o' in front of a masculine singular noun:
> | bueno, buen | Hace buen tiempo. |
> | malo, mal | Hace mal tiempo. |
> | primero, primer | el primer ministro |
> | tercero, tercer | el tercer piso |
> | alguno, algún | algún día |
> | ninguno, ningún | ningún deporte |

## 2 Position

Some adjectives change their meaning according to their position, **mismo** and **pobre** being common examples:

| Es el mismo vestido. | = It's the same dress. |
| Yo mismo/a voy. | = I'm going myself. |
| Pobre Miguel. | = Poor Miguel. |
| Es un país pobre. | = It's a poor country. |

**Grande** loses its **-de** when in front of any singular noun and in this case it changes its meaning from 'big' to 'great'.

| Picasso es un gran pintor. | = Picasso is a great painter. |
| Ciudad de México es una ciudad grande. | = Mexico City is a big city. |

## 3 Possessive Adjectives

The words for 'my', 'your', 'his' and 'her' are the same for both masculine and feminine. You add an 's' to make them plural:

| | SINGULAR | | PLURAL | |
|---|---|---|---|---|
| | Masculine/Feminine | | Masculine/Feminine | |
| my your (tú) his/her your (usted) | **mi** libro **tu** cuaderno **su** bolígrafo | | **mis** libros **tus** cuadernos **sus** bolígrafos | |
| | Masculine | Feminine | Masculine | Feminine |
| our your | **nuestro** ordenador **vuestro** ordenador | **nuestra** casa **vuestra** casa | **nuestros** pupitres **vuestros** pupitres | **nuestras** sillas **vuestras** sillas |
| | Masculine/Feminine | | Masculine/Feminine | |
| their/your (ustedes) | **su** dormitorio | | **sus** dormitorios | |

## 4 Demonstrative Adjectives

The words for 'this', 'these', 'that', 'those' and 'that/those over there' agree with the nouns they describe:

| MASCULINE | PLURAL |
|---|---|
| **este** sombrero | **estos** sombreros |
| **ese** abrigo | **esos** abrigos |
| **aquel** jersey | **aquellos** jerseys |

| FEMININE | PLURAL |
|---|---|
| **esta** camisa | **estas** camisas |
| **esa** bufanda | **esas** bufandas |
| **aquella** corbata | **aquellas** botas |

> **For your own notes**
> .................................................
> .................................................
> .................................................
> .................................................
> .................................................
> .................................................

# ADVERBS

## 1 Adverbs as Quantifiers

To describe quantity and degree, use quantifiers. These are some examples:

| | | |
|---|---|---|
| muy | Es muy rico. = It's very tasty. | |
| poco | Tengo poco dinero. = I don't have much money. | |
| mucho | Hizo mucho frío. = It was very cold. | |
| demasiado | He bebido demasiado. = I have drunk too much. | |
| bastante | He comido bastante. = I have eaten enough. | |

## 2 Formation and Gender

Take the feminine form of the adjective and add -**mente**. E.g. básica – básicamente.

> **Watch out for this exception!**
> Some adverbs don't end in -**mente**. E.g. bien, mal, despacio.

If two adverbs are used together, -**mente** is added only to the second one. E.g. Trabaja rápida e inteligentemente.

## 3 Comparatives and Superlatives

barato/a = cheap

rápido/a = fast

más barato/a = cheaper

más rápido/a = faster

el/la más barato/a = the cheapest

el/la más rápido/a = the fastest

| | |
|---|---|
| Belén es más alta que José. | = Belén is taller than José. |
| Los precios más baratos de la ciudad. | = The cheapest prices in town. |

**Menos** translates as 'less' or 'not so':

| | |
|---|---|
| Es menos caro. | = It is less expensive. |

**Tan ... como** translates as 'as ... as ...':

| | |
|---|---|
| Es tan bonita como tú. | = She's as pretty as you. |

**Más ... que** translates as 'more ... than ...'

| | |
|---|---|
| Ir en tren es más cómodo que ir en autocar. | = Going by train is more comfortable than going by coach. |

**Más de** and **menos de** translate as 'more/less than' and are used with numbers:

| | |
|---|---|
| Más de mil personas acudieron al concierto. | = More than 1000 people went to the concert. |

| | |
|---|---|
| Menos de 50 por ciento de la clase aprobaron el examen. | = Less than 50 per cent of the class passed the exam. |

**BEWARE!**

There are two special forms of grande, depending on the meaning:

| | |
|---|---|
| grande = big | grande = great |
| más grande = bigger | mayor = greater, older (age only) |
| el más grande = the biggest | |
| el mayor = the greatest, the oldest (age only) | |

> **Watch out for these irregular adverbs!**
>
> | | |
> |---|---|
> | bien = well | mal = bad |
> | mejor = better | peor = worse |
> | el mejor = the best | el peor = the worst |
> | mucho = much | poco = little |
> | más = more | menos = less |
> | el más = the most | el menos = the least |

-**ísimo** at the end of an adjective translates as 'very', 'most'. E.g. corto – cortísimo, bueno – buenísimo, rico – riquísimo. (Note the spelling changes.)

## 4 Diminutives

These are used to indicate smallness. They are formed by adding either of these endings:

-**ito** (-cito, -ecito, -ececito) and -**illo** (-cillo, -ecillo, -ececillo).

- -**ito** is the most common and can also indicate affection:

| | |
|---|---|
| Juan | Juanito |
| señora | señorita |
| pueblo | pueblecito |
| cuchara | cucharita |

## 5 Augmentatives

These are used less than diminutives:

-**ón, -ona** is the most common and indicates an increase in size or quality.

-**azo, -uza** indicates disproportionate size.

-**ote, -ota** is usually used to make something appear monstrous or ridiculous.

| | |
|---|---|
| guapo | guapetón |
| gente | gentuza |

# PRONOUNS

## 1 Demonstrative Pronouns

These follow the same pattern as demonstrative adjectives, but notice the accents:

MASCULINE | PLURAL
--- | ---
**éste** es mi tío | **éstos** son mis tíos
**ése** es mi abuelo | **ésos** son mis abuelos
**aquél** es mi padre | **aquéllos** son mis padres

FEMININE | PLURAL
--- | ---
**ésta** es mi prima | **éstas** son mis primas
**ésa** es mi hermana | **ésas** son mis hermanas
**aquélla** es mi sobrina | **aquéllas** son mis sobrinas

## 2 Relative Pronouns

'Who', 'what' and 'that' translate as **que**. 'Whom' translates as **que** or **a quien(es)**:

El tren que va a Sevilla. = The train that goes to Seville.

'Whose' is translated as **cuyo/a/s**:

El amigo cuya moto voy a comprar. = The friend whose motorbike I am going to buy.

'Which' after a preposition is expressed in either of the following ways:

| Masculine singular | Masculine plural | Feminine singular | Feminine plural |
| --- | --- | --- | --- |
| **el que** **el cual** | **los que** **los cuales** | **la que** **la cual** | **las que** **las cuales** |

It agrees with the noun to which it refers:

¿Cuáles son tus bolsas? = Which are your bags?

**Lo que** translates as 'what' in the middle of a sentence:

Sé lo que están diciendo. = I know what they are saying.

## 3 Subject Pronouns

| SINGULAR | | PLURAL | | |
| --- | --- | --- | --- | --- |
| | | Masculine | Feminine | |
| yo | I | nosotros (m) | nosotras (f) | we |
| tú (familiar) | you | vosotros (m) | vosotras (f) | you |
| él | he/it | ellos (m) | ellas (f) | they |
| ella | she/it | | | |
| usted | you (polite) | ustedes | ustedes | you (polite) |

## 4 Direct Object Pronouns

| SINGULAR | | PLURAL | |
| --- | --- | --- | --- |
| me | me | nos | us |
| te | you | os | you |
| le/lo | you (polite)/him/it | les/los | them/you (polite) |
| la | you (polite)/her/it | las | them/you (polite) |

## 5 Indirect Object Pronouns

| SINGULAR | | PLURAL | |
| --- | --- | --- | --- |
| me | to me | nos | to us |
| te | to you | os | to you |
| le | to you (polite)/him/her/it | les | to them/you (polite) |

The object pronouns are placed immediately before the verb:

Lo compra. = He buys it.
Nos hablan. = They speak to us.
No te comprendo. = I don't understand you.

The object pronoun is joined on to the end of the verb in certain cases:

- infinitives: Viene a verlo. = He is coming to see it.
- present participles: Estoy comiéndolo. = I am eating it.
- commands: Escuchadme. = Listen to me.

When two object pronouns are together – one direct, the other indirect – the indirect always goes before the direct:

Va a dármelo. = He is going to give it to me.
Explíquemelo. = Explain it to me.

When **le** or **les** comes before **lo, la, los** and **las,** you change the **le** or **les** to **se:**

Se lo doy. = I give it to him.

When two verbs are together, with the second one in the infinitive, object pronouns can either be put on the end of the infinitive or placed in front of the verb:

Se la voy a prestar. OR Voy a prestársela. = I am going to lend it to him.

## 6 Possessive Pronouns

|  | SINGULAR | |
|---|---|---|
|  | Masculine | Feminine |
| mine | el mío | la mía |
| yours | el tuyo | la tuya |
| his/hers/yours (polite) | el suyo | la suya |
| ours | el nuestro | la nuestra |
| yours (plural) | el vuestro | la vuestra |
| theirs/yours (polite plural) | el suyo | la suya |
|  | PLURAL | |
|  | Masculine | Feminine |
| mine | los míos | las mías |
| yours | los tuyos | las tuyas |
| his/hers/yours (polite) | los suyos | las suyas |
| ours | los nuestros | las nuestras |
| yours (plural) | los vuestros | las vuestras |
| theirs/yours (polite plural) | los suyos | las suyas |

**El (Los)/La(s) suyo/a/s** have six possible meanings. To avoid confusion, they can be replaced by **de él, de ella, de Vd, de ellos, de ellas, de Vds**:

No me gusta su chaqueta.    = I don't like his jacket.
Prefiero la de ella.    I prefer hers.

When the possessive pronoun comes immediately after a part of ser, you leave out the definite article:

Esa bolsa es suya.    = That bag is his.
OR Esa bolsa es de él.

## 7 Strong Pronouns

| mí | me | nosotros | us |
|---|---|---|---|
| ti | you | vosotros | you (plural) |
| él | him/it | ellos | them (masculine) |
| ella | her/it | ellas | them (feminine) |
| Vd | you (polite) | Vds | you (polite plural) |
| sí * | oneself | | |

para mí = for me

con ellos = with them

\*   Sí is not commonly used but it is useful to recognise it. It means: oneself, himself, herself, yourself (formal); themselves, yourselves (formal) when it refers back to the subject of the sentence.

Estaba fuera de sí.    = She was beside herself (with worry).

# PREPOSITIONS

**a la derecha de** = to the right of

**a la izquierda de** = to the left of

**dentro de** = inside    **detrás de** = behind

**al lado de** = next to    **enfrente de** = opposite

**debajo de** = under    **fuera de** = outside

**delante de** = in front of    **sobre** = on top of

El banco está al lado del supermercado.    = The bank is next to the supermarket.

Remember that **a + el** becomes **al**, and that **de + el** becomes **del**.

- **desde** = since

This is used with the present tense in Spanish where in English you would use the perfect tense:

Estoy aquí desde las 9h 00.    = I have been here since 9.00.

- **desde hace** = for

¿Desde hace cuánto tiempo estudias español?    = How long have you been studying Spanish?

Estudio español desde hace tres años.    = I have been studying Spanish for three years.

- **acabar de** = to have just

This is followed by a verb in the infinitive:

Acabamos de mudarnos de casa.    = We have just moved house.

# NUMBERS

- **Uno** becomes **un** before a masculine noun: Un hermano.

- **Cien** becomes **ciento** when it is followed or preceded by another number:

  **Cien** gramos de jamón serrano. **Ciento** cincuenta gramos de chorizo.

- To name a year in Spanish, you do not break up the number of the year into two as in English:

  mil cuatrocientos noventa y dos = 1492

- **Primero** becomes **primer** before a masculine noun: el primer piso.

  **Primera** remains the same: la primera vez.

- **Dates**

  el primero/dos/tres de mayo = (May 1st/2nd/3rd)

## Ordinal Numbers

| | | | | | |
|---|---|---|---|---|---|
| 1º/ª | primero/a | 6º/ª | sexto/a | | |
| 2º/ª | segundo/a | 7º/ª | séptimo/a | | |
| 3º/ª | tercero/a | 8º/ª | octavo/a | | |
| 4º/ª | cuarto/a | 9º/ª | noveno/a | | |
| 5º/ª | quinto/a | 10º/ª | décimo/a | | |

$1^0$ = el primero (m)/$1^a$ = la primera (f) = first

el último (m)/la última (f) = last

Ordinal numbers after 10th are rarely used in Spanish. Instead you use the cardinal numbers after the noun. E.g. el siglo veintiuno = the 21st century.

# WRITING

## 1 Spelling Changes

Certain rules in Spanish cause changes in the spelling of words, particularly with verbs:

**z** changes to **c** when followed by **e** or **i**.

Crucé la calle. = I crossed the street.

**g** changes to **gu** when followed by **e** or **i**.

Pagué la cuenta. = I paid the bill.

**c** (hard) changes to **qu** when followed by **e** or **i**.

No te acerques al fuego. = Don't go near the fire.

**g** (soft) changes to **j** when not followed by **e** or **i**.

Coja el tren. = Get/catch the train.

**gu** changes to **g** when not followed by **e** or **i**.

Siga por la calle. = Carry on down the street.

**i** changes to **y** when it is unstressed and comes between two vowels

Cayó al suelo. = It fell on the floor.

## 2 Accents

The accent on an **ñ/Ñ** indicates that you must pronounce the n as 'ny'. The only other accent in Spanish is like the acute accent, e.g. ú. Follow these rules when deciding whether to use an accent:

- If a word ends in a vowel, **n** or **s**, the stress falls on the last but one syllable. E.g. buscamos, hablas, mesa, preguntan, pupitre, trabajaba.
- If the word ends in a consonant (apart from **n** or **s**), the stress is on the last syllable: andaluz, azul, desayunar, escuchad, Madrid, venir.
- If the pronunciation of the word means that either of the above rules is broken, an accent must be placed over the stressed vowel. E.g. bailó, buzón, comía, francés, película, vendría.
- Question words: ¿cómo?, ¿cuál?, ¿cuándo?, ¿cuántos?, ¿qué?, ¿quién?.

- When two words with different meanings are spelt the same, one of them carries an accent:

sí = yes, si = if

mí = me, mi = my

él = him, el = the

Congratulations! Have you worked through the ten topics chapters, the word lists and the grammar reference section? And how did you do in the mock exam in Chapter 12? If you have made the most of this Spanish Revision Guide you will be able to do your best in the GCSE exam.

So if your exam is tomorrow have a bath now and relax. Make sure you are feeling calm about the exam. As a last boost why not browse through the word lists in this book and look at the lists and the diagrams you have drawn yourself. Good luck!

### For your own notes